RACERS

COW PONY

PLOUGHING

JUMPER

CIRCUS

POLICE

THE *REAL BOOK* ABOUT

Horses

THE *REAL BOOK* ABOUT

Horses

by

JAY SHERMAN

Illustrated by Lumen Winter

EDITED BY HELEN HOKE

Garden City Books

GARDEN CITY, NEW YORK

BY ARRANGEMENT WITH FRANKLIN WATTS, INC.

1952
GARDEN CITY BOOKS

PRINTED IN THE UNITED STATES

To Ned

Contents

Introduction   11

Part 1 HORSES OF LONG AGO   15
        MAN FIRST USES THE HORSE   18
        THE HORSE GOES TO WAR   20
        KNIGHTS AND THEIR HORSES   22
        THE HORSE RETURNS TO AMERICA   26

Part 2 HORSE TALK   31

Part 3 HORSES OF TODAY   37
        FROM A-MERICAN SADDLE HORSE TO
            Z-EBRA   37
        HEAVY DRAFT BREEDS   38
            Belgian   38
            Clydesdale   40
            Percheron   41
            Shire   43
            Suffolk   45
        TOUGH AND SHAGGY BREEDS   45
            Wild Horses of Asia   45
            Norwegian Dun   46
            Shetland Pony   47
        SLENDER AND RAPID BREEDS   50
            American Saddle Horse   50

7

EARLY CARE AND TRAINING
   OF A SADDLE HORSE 53
   Arabian 56
   Hackney 60
   Morgan 62
   Quarter Horse 64
   Standardbred 66
   Tennessee Walking Horse 69
   Thoroughbred 71
ALMOST BREEDS 72
   Hunter 73
   Mustang 74
   Polo Pony 77
   Palomino 78
ALMOST HORSES 80
   Donkey 80
   Mule 82
   Zebra 84

Part 4 HORSES AT WORK 87
   WAR HORSES 87
   TRAIL AND PACK HORSES 89
   CONESTOGA HORSES 91
   CANALBOAT HORSES 93
   COACH HORSES 94
   TRAIN AND STREETCAR HORSES 98
   PONY EXPRESS 100
   FARM HORSES 104
   COW HORSES 106
   FIRE HORSES 111
   POLICE HORSES 113
   CITY HORSES TODAY 116

Part 5 HORSES AT PLAY 117
    CHARIOT HORSES 117
    POLO 119
    STEEPLECHASE 123
    FOX HUNTING 125
    RACING 128
        Flat Racing 128
        Harness Racing 134
    CIRCUS HORSES 138
    RODEO 142
    HORSE SHOWS AND STATE FAIRS 145
    RIDING FOR PLEASURE 149

Part 6 HORSES RARE AND DIFFERENT 152
    HORSE SENSE IN GENERAL 152
    OUTSTANDING HORSES 157

Part 7 HORSES AND YOU 163
    SO YOU WANT TO OWN A HORSE! 163
    YOU GIVE YOUR HORSE A NAME
        AND A HOME 165
    TINKER'S DIET 166
    TINKER'S GOOD LOOKS 167
    TINKER'S WARDROBE 169
    YOU LEARN TO RIDE TINKER 170
    UP YOU GET! 172
    THE SEAT 174
    THE HANDS 175
    AIDS 176
    THE DIFFERENT GAITS 177
        The Walk 178
        The Trot 180

The Canter	181
The Gallop	181
Down You Get!	182
Your Riding Habit	183
Fun with Tinker	184
MORE BOOKS TO READ	187
INDEX	189

10

Introduction

"A horse! A horse! My kingdom for a horse!"

So cried Shakespeare's king, Richard III of England long ago. And so today, many boys and girls have cried to themselves, "A horse! A horse! What wouldn't I give to own a horse!"

Maybe you are a lucky one who has a pony, or who lives on a farm or a ranch with horses all around you. More likely you live in a city or town where the closest you ever come to a horse is in the books you read, or the movies, TV shows and circuses you see. Yet whether they are part of your daily life or only part of your amusements, horses probably have the same fascination for you that they've had for generations of girls and boys.

The story is told that when the present Princess Elizabeth of England was only six years old she was walking one day with her grandmother Queen Mary. She didn't seem to be paying much attention to the conversation, so Queen Mary asked her what she was thinking about. Elizabeth looked across the park to a pasture where some colts were capering. "I was thinking," she answered, "that if I weren't a princess I'd like to be a horse."

Why do you suppose horses have this great fascination for us? In these days planes, cars or streamlined trains can take people comfortably and quickly wherever they

11

want to go. Tractors plow most fields, tanks have taken the place of cavalry, while trucks are used instead of wagons. One might think the horse was no longer necessary at all.

Yet according to the *World Almanac* for 1950 there were 7,463,000 horses and mules working on the farms of the United States alone. This means there are about 10,000,000 horses of different kinds in America today. And more valuable horses than in any other entire country are raised in the area that is made up of Illinois, Iowa, Nebraska, Kansas, southern Minnesota and the eastern part of the Dakotas.

So horses still perform important work in the Machine Age. They patrol city streets and parks as police horses. They plow some of the fields to help raise the wheat that makes bread. They carry to market a lot of the cotton that makes clothes. On western ranches they round up all the cattle that provide beef and leather. They haul carts from truck farms to deliver fruits and vegetables to market.

In addition, human beings get a great deal of pleasure and entertainment from horses that perform in rodeos, circuses and movies. Thousands cheer them at races, polo games, steeplechases or horse shows. People who own horses enjoy their companionship through the exercise of riding. These may be some of the reasons why you are fascinated by this faithful animal friend.

THE *REAL BOOK* ABOUT

Horses

PART 1

Horses of Long Ago

It took many, many thousands of years for man and horse to become friends. Everything is not definitely known about the horse's history, but enough has been accurately traced to get a pretty clear picture of how horses grew up to be the helpers they are today.

From skeletons found in Wyoming, New Mexico and other parts of the world, scientists discovered three things about the earliest-known horses in the world:

1. They lived on the earth some forty million years ago —millions of years before the first men appeared on the scene.

2. They were the size of a small dog, the largest ones standing about twenty inches high and weighing less than one hundred pounds.

3. They lived in North America, then disappeared from that continent until they were brought back here many thousands of years later.

The first horse is called Eohippus, or the Dawn horse. He was probably given this pretty name because he lived at the dawn of a new era, the Age of Mammals. Mammals are animals that suckle their babies on their own milk. The little Dawn horse can proudly claim to be one of the very first mammals.

He came into the world right after the enormous dinosaurs had killed each other all off. This was a lucky thing for the horse, since otherwise he would surely have been destroyed by these huge monsters. It is amazing enough that such a tiny, tender creature managed to survive among the other large prehistoric animals that still existed.

For the Dawn horse had no natural weapons with which to protect himself from his enemies. His body was small, round and rather fat. His little teeth were just sharp enough to nibble grass with. He had only one way to save his life when it was in danger. He could run through the great forests faster than almost any other animal then living.

But in those days he didn't have hoofs as modern horses have. He had four toes on each front foot and three on each back foot. These toes were padded, like a dog's foot, and had strong nails. The pads made it possible for the small horse to escape without making any noise. The toes helped him grip uneven ground, while the toenails helped him climb over hills and rocks.

The Dawn horse probably ran on the tips of his toes to get away from his enemies quickly and quietly. He threw his weight on his center toe as he ran. Little by little, over many thousands of years, this toe on each foot became stronger than the other toes. The toes that weren't used grew weaker and smaller until finally, after generations had passed, they entirely disappeared. The toenails on the remaining center toes grew bigger and harder with rough wear. Gradually, one huge nail surrounded the whole toe on each foot—and this is how the horse got his hoofs.

North America was still connected by land to Asia in these times. Some scientists believe that horses first came to this continent from Asia. Others think that the Dawn horse originated in what is now America, then wandered up to Alaska and over a land bridge to the steppes of Siberia and down to Europe.

Wherever they came from, however, they did live here a long time. Their bodies grew larger and they began to have bigger teeth as they developed hoofs in place of toes. Then they all disappeared from this continent—no one knows exactly why.

One group of historians thinks it happened when the Ice Age began to freeze some of the green grass, trees and other vegetation. Horses started then to travel away from cold and hunger to look for a warmer home and better food. They went across to Asia, down into Europe and even as far as Africa in this search. By the time the great glaciers finally covered the North American continent there were no horses left on its surface.

Another group of historians believes that the reason all the horses disappeared from this part of the world was because they were killed by some disease. But however it really happened, there were no horses in America for many, many thousands of years.

It may seem cruel that the very first way man used the horse was to eat him. Piles of colts' bones, cracked so the marrow could be sucked out, have been found in European caves where primitive men once lived. This has caused most experts to agree that long before man tamed the horse he killed him for food.

After horses left America they continued to grow bigger and stronger. Countless numbers of them roamed the forests and plains of Europe and Asia. Man had to kill animals in order to feed his family in these early days of his history. So when he saw lions or tigers devouring horses he, too, decided they might make a good food. This was long before he had learned the many other ways a horse could aid him, remember. The small wild horses he killed were no more his friends or helpers than were the other animals he ate then.

Horses continued to be eaten even long after men became civilized. The early colonists brought horses with them from England to Virginia. When starvation threatened to wipe out their settlement at Jamestown they ate most of their horses. To this very day it is the custom in many parts of the world to eat horse meat as Americans eat beef, pork or lamb. And even in the United States the hoofs of horses and calves are used to make the gelatin that in turn makes some desserts. Horse meat is also used to feed dogs and as food for animals kept in zoos.

But early man soon found that the horse could be valuable to him in other ways. When he noticed how fast this particular animal could run, he began to wonder how he could use this speed to help him get places quickly.

Early man soon found that the horse could be valuable to him

He didn't dream of jumping up on a horse's back and riding him, however. The idea never occurred to him for the simple reason that horses then stood only about four feet high and were not strong enough to carry men on their backs. But man had been using slow, sluggish oxen to pull his carts for quite a while. He had also domesticated sheep, goats, pigs and dogs, so he knew how to tame wild animals. Now he decided to tame horses and harness them to his rough chariots.

But taming a placid ox and taming a spirited wild horse were two very different things. Once man caught a horse, the big problem was how to control him and get him to go where he wanted him to go. It must have been then that man discovered an important fact about how a horse's teeth grow. He found that there was a space between the horse's canine teeth and back teeth. He next

19

found that if he placed a small bar of iron in this space—across the horse's mouth—and then attached this bar to rope lines, he could turn the horse's head from one side to the other by pulling on one or the other of the ropes. This bar, which is now called a bit, and the unusual space between a horse's teeth are what made it possible for man to guide and control the horse. The discovery of these things marked the beginning of the many ways the horse has helped man, from primitive days right up to now.

The Horse Goes to War

After man once tamed him, the horse's physical and useful development was rapid. Probably the first way this tame horse helped man was in his wars.

As early as 2000 B.C. the Assyrians harnessed their horses to bronze chariots which carried soldiers who wore armor. A little later, horses had grown into such large, strong animals that the soldiers of ancient Egypt and Greece began to ride on their backs. Alexander the Great of Greece used war horses so skillfully that he became one of the most famous of all the world's warriors. There is a story which tells how Alexander tamed his equally famous horse:

Alexander was only thirteen years old when someone gave his father a beautiful black horse with a white star on his forehead. This horse was so fiery that his father wanted to send him away. But the boy fell in love with the spirited animal and begged to be allowed to try to tame him.

One of the things young Alexander had noticed was

that the horse seemed to be terribly frightened and enraged by his own shadow. So the boy turned him to face the sun. That way the horse couldn't see any shadows. Holding onto the reins, Alexander whispered to the horse as he gently stroked him. When the animal calmed down a bit Alexander jumped up on his back. Without using whip or spurs, he clung to the galloping horse until he stopped bucking.

His father allowed the clever boy to keep the horse, which was named Bucephalus. From that day on, Bucephalus served Alexander faithfully and courageously. Alexander loved him so much that when Bucephalus died —many, many years later—he ordered that a city be built in India named Bucephala. In the very center of the city stood the horse's gold and alabaster tomb.

The Greeks believed that Apollo's chariot, drawn by galloping steeds across the sky from east to west, was the sun. Pegasus, the winged horse who could fly, was another of their gods. And the centaurs, those odd little creatures who were supposed to be half man and half horse, appear in many old Greek tales.

Norsemen in their cold lands had their own horse myths, too. They believed that young women warriors, called Valkyrie, rode down from the sky to pick up the bodies of fallen soldiers and carry them to Valhalla, the heaven of heroes. They called these Valkyrie on their steeds the northern lights.

On the other side of the world the Chinese began to use horses around 1000 B.C. For a time these people were conquered by one of the greatest invasions in all history, the conquest of Genghis Khan and his Tartars. Genghis Khan led his army of seven hundred thousand horsemen from the steppes of Asia deep into the heart of China and as far west as the Dnieper River in Russia.

These Tartar soldiers were Mongolians who made their living in peaceful days by being a sort of cowboy of those times. They rounded up great herds of goats and sheep with their shaggy Mongolian ponies. They thought a horse was their equal, for without him they could not have existed. When they joined Genghis Khan they rode horseback and carried bows and arrows.

One of the rules Genghis Khan laid down for his army was "Never strike a horse." And his ponies responded to this kind treatment. They bravely did what was demanded of them. They swam the swiftest rivers and galloped over the roughest country. Because they had longer noses than most other horses, they could keep themselves from starving even in the hardest winter. They sniffed under the snow to eat the moss that grew there. They were strong enough to stand both the bitter Siberian cold and the fierce summer sun of Asia. Without these faithful, tough little animals it is doubtful if Genghis Khan could have accomplished his great conquest.

In Japan the horse was treated as a sacred animal. He was kept in a brightly painted temple stall, where he was fed delicacies. Until the Americans came to Japan about a hundred years ago, the horse was never used as a work animal by the Japanese.

KNIGHTS AND THEIR HORSES

Moving up in time, and over to the British Isles, we come to the age of knighthood. England had its own

*The charger was a large, powerful horse which the knight
rode in tournaments*

breeds of horses even before Caesar came to that country. Caesar brought his Roman horses with him, however. These two kinds of horses probably mated to produce the strong, heavy breeds that the knights needed much later. By that time horses had developed into the size they now are.

Knights were not only soldiers but also defenders of their religious faith, their king and their lovely ladies. The time in which they lived was called the Age of Chivalry. And the word "chivalry" comes from the French word *cheval*—which means horse! A chivalrous knight just had to be a horseman.

The knights fought wars for their king, went on crusades to far lands for their religion, jousted for the honor of their sweethearts. To do all these things a proper knight needed more than one horse. He usually had four. One was his charger. This was a large, powerful horse— as he had to be in order to carry his master when he wore his full suit of armor. The charger was the horse knights used in tournaments, such at those described in Sir Walter Scott's book *Ivanhoe*.

The second horse was called a palfrey. The knight rode from place to place—without wearing his armor—on this smaller, lighter horse. It had an easier gait than the big charger for long trips. If the knight was on his way to a tournament he tied the charger to the palfrey, trailing the larger mount along behind.

The third and most important horse was the courser. This was the mount the knight rode into battle. He was the fastest of the four and the one used most in jousts. This is the horse that is written about in stories of King Arthur.

The courser was the mount the knight rode into battle

The fourth horse was called a battle horse, but in reality he was just a pack animal. He carried the knight's weapons, extra shields, baggage and armor when the knight went to war or on a crusade. The knight never rode this lowly creature.

The Horse Returns to America

When knighthood died out in Europe a new kind of adventurer appeared on the scene—the sailor-explorer. Perhaps the most famous of these was Christopher Columbus. When he sailed to discover America he brought five mares and twenty stallions with him to the West Indies.

Small, spirited horses called Barbs had been brought to Spain in 710—with the invasion of the Moors from North Africa. These desert horses mated with larger native Spanish horses, and from 1200 to 1600 Spain raised the best horses in all Europe. This was the kind of horse that Columbus brought with him. On later trips to the West Indies Spanish colonists brought more horses and raised them there.

When Cortes sailed from Cuba to invade Mexico in 1519, he took with him sixteen or eighteen of these horses. And they were the first horses to set foot on the American continent since prehistoric days.

Later, reinforcements brought as many as a thousand horses to help Cortes conquer the Aztecs. Some of these animals escaped from their owners and roamed north to what is now Texas. De Soto brought about a hundred horses to Florida in 1539. They carried the explorer and

*Cortes brought with him the first horses to set foot in America
since prehistoric days*

his men as far inland as the Mississippi River. But after they crossed the river some of these horses ran away, too. Out on the western plains the Cortes runaways met and mated with the De Soto runaways. They had so many foals that only a short time later, around 1580, the Indians were capturing, taming and riding descendants of the original Spanish horses.

These were called wild horses because they wandered around the countryside completely on their own. But they were not truly wild. Real wild horses are those which have never in all their history been tamed by men. The only true remaining ones today are the wild horses of Asia and the zebras of Africa. American "wild" horses are what is called "feral." This means they are the descendants of horses that had once been domesticated, but who were left to run wild and feed themselves. When caught and tamed by the Indians they were called cayuses. Later, when our cowboys began to use them on the ranges, they were known as mustangs. A bronco is simply one of those wild mustangs which has not been broken.

The Spanish horses roamed over what is now our Southwest. They later became the wonderful cow ponies, without which the great cattle-raising industry could never have been built.

Indians were the first men to tame the descendants of the Spanish horses. American Indians had never seen a horse until the Spaniards brought them to their land. Like the Gauchos down in South America, however, they quickly saw the value of this strange animal—and became the best horse breeders of the time. They soon learned how to "break" a wild horse so he could be ridden.

It took a lot of skill and understanding to do this. Several Indians roped a wild horse and held him. The Indian who was to be the trainer talked to the horse from a distance. He used a deep chest tone as he repeated "Hoh! Hoh!" (This is where we got the word "whoa" to stop a horse.) Then the trainer waved a blanket at the horse. At first the animal was terrified by this. But once he learned that the blanket did not hurt him, he calmed down. Only then did the Indian draw near enough to put a hand on the horse's nose. Talking softly all the time, he came closer and closer until the horse let himself be touched.

Then the trainer could put a simple bridle on the horse's head. Holding onto a rope attached to the bridle —talking, hissing, reassuring the frightened animal—the Indian little by little petted his back, head and shoulders. Later he touched his flanks, finally his legs and feet. After many days of this patient handling, the time came when the trainer could put a blanket on the horse's back. Once this was done without scaring the horse, it was comparatively easy to ride him. The horses which were trained in this slow, careful way by Indians seldom bucked—even when they were mounted for the very first time.

Indians became expert horsemen, riding over hills and plains without saddle, bridle or stirrups. They made the horse their friend and companion because they depended on his speed to help them kill the buffalo, their main source of food. They twisted horsehair into ropes. They used horsehide to make their beds, clothes, tents, saddles and moccasins.

The Indians treated their horses with kindness, respect and intelligence. The Comanches, Navahos and Cheyennes were said to be the best of all Indian horsemen.

They judged how wealthy a man was by how many horses he owned. They tested their leaders by their skill in handling horses. The Pueblo Indians of New Mexico valued the horse so highly that when one of their chiefs died they dressed his favorite horses in fine trappings, then killed them at the Chief's grave. They thought that the horses would go with their master to the Great Spirit.

PART 2

Horse Talk

There are many special words used when horse lovers get together to discuss their favorite subject. Here are the definitions of some of these words to help you understand such "horse talk" when you hear or read it.

ACTION: the movement of a horse's feet and legs

AIDS: signals given to his horse by a rider, usually with hands, legs and body

BALKING: horse's refusal to move on order

BARREL: body of a horse between front and rear legs

BAY: a coat color that shades from red-gold to dark liver, with black legs below the hocks

BIT: the metal part of the bridle which goes in a horse's mouth, to which reins are attached

BLAZE: a white mark on a horse's face

BREAK: to tame or train a horse

BREED: that particular horse family to which a horse belongs

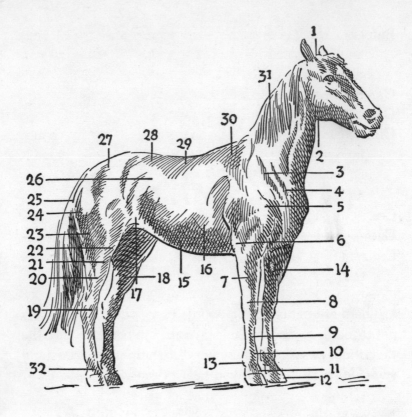

1. Poll	12. Foot	22. Thigh
2. Throat	13. Fetlock tuft and	23. Buttock
3. Shoulder	ergot	24. Point of Buttock
4. Point of shoulder	14. Forearm	25. Tail
5. Arm	15. Belly	26. Point of haunch
6. Elbow	16. Chest	27. Point of croup
7. Chestnut	17. Flank	28. Loin
8. Knee	18. Gaskin	29. Back
9. Cannon	19. Hock	30. Withers
10. Fetlock	20. Leg	31. Neck
11. Coronet	21. Stifle	32. Pastern

BRIDLE: the head harness by which a horse is controlled, consisting of leather headstall and reins and metal bit

CANTER: a gait that is a slow, three-beat gallop

CANTLE: the rear bow of a saddle

CHESTNUT: a reddish-brown coat color, with mane and tail usually the same shade. A light chestnut horse is called a "sorrel." A dark one is called a "liver chestnut"

COLT: a young male horse

CROP: a short, stiff riding whip

CRUPPER: a leather loop that passes under the horse's tail

CURB: a bit shaped like the letter H

CURRYCOMB: a metal comb used to remove dirt from a horse's coat

DAM: a mother horse

DOCKED: when a horse's tail has been cut short he is said to have been "docked"

DRAFT HORSE: a horse of any heavy breed that is used to pull heavy loads

DUN: a coat color shading from mouse gray to sandy, often with a darker stripe down the back

EQUITATION: the art of horseback riding

FILLY: a female horse under three years old

FOAL: a colt or filly under nine months old

FOREHAND: that part of the horse's body that is in front of the saddle

GAIT: the way a horse moves, such as walk, trot, etc.

GALLOP: the fastest gait, where both front feet and both back feet move together. There is a moment in the gallop when all four feet are off the ground

GELDING: a male horse that has been altered so he has no sex

GIRTH: the band attached to the saddle which reaches around the horse's body and holds the saddle in place

GRAY: a smoky coat color. A horse with a dark gray coat is called "steel gray." A gray coat with white in it is called "dappled." Gray foals are usually black at birth and white when they grow old

GROOM: one who takes care of a horse's appearance

GROOMING: the care given to a horse's appearance

HALTER: a rope attached to leather straps around a horse's head. Used for leading

HAND: the term used in measuring the height of a horse. A hand is equal to four inches

HARNESS HORSE: a horse of any light breed that has been trained to pull a carriage

HOGGED: a horse is said to be "hogged" when his mane is cropped close to his neck, leaving only a stiff crest of hair

MARE: a female horse over three years old

MARTINGALE: a leather strap running from the noseband down between the legs to the girth. It prevents the horse from throwing his head up or holding it too high

MOUNT: a riding horse. To get up on a horse

NECK REINING: to guide a horse by laying the reins on the side of his neck opposite the direction you want him to go

PAINT: a horse with a coat that is white with uneven patches of other colors. Also called a pinto

PIEBALD: a horse with a coat that has black and white patches of different sizes

PINTO: the Spanish word meaning "paint." Same as a paint horse

PLEASURE HORSE: a horse used for his owner's enjoyment, such as riding or driving

POINTING: when a horse rests a forefoot he is said to be "pointing." Usually a sign of lameness

RACK: a speedy, four-beat, man-taught gait. Not one of the natural gaits

REARING: when a horse rises on his two hind legs he is said to be "rearing"

REINS: the control lines of leather that are attached to the bit and held in the rider's or driver's hands

ROAN: a coat where white hairs are evenly mixed throughout a solid color. A strawberry roan has a chestnut coat mixed with white hairs. A red roan has a bay coat with white hairs

RUNNING WALK: a fast, four-beat walk, with opposite front and back feet moving at the same time. The back feet often step ahead of the prints left by the front feet

SCOPE: the ability of a horse to extend his legs in order to take a wide jump

SHOES: iron, U-shaped articles fitted and nailed to a horse's hoofs to protect them

SHYING: when a horse jumps away from something he fears he is said to be "shying"

SIRE: a father horse

SKEWBALD: a horse that is white with any color, except black, making different-sized patches

SNAFFLE: a type of bit that is jointed in the center

SOUND: a horse is said to be "sound" when he is free from blemishes and in good health and condition

STABLE: a building used to house livestock

STALL: the part of the stable in which a horse is kept

STALLION: a full-grown male horse

STAR: a small white mark on a horse's face

STOCK HORSE: a horse trained to drive, cut out and round up cattle on a range

STRIDE: the length of a horse's step made by one foot moving forward

STUD HORSE: a stallion used only for breeding purposes

TACK: all the equipment used for a horse in riding or driving, including saddle, buggy, bit, reins, etc.

TROT: a smart, fast, two-beat gait where the opposite front and back feet move at the same time

WAY OF GOING: the way a horse moves

WEANLING: a six-month-old foal that has been taken away from his mother to learn to eat solid food

WELL-BRED: said of a horse that shows the clear characteristics of his breed

YAWNING: when a horse reaches down and out with his mouth, he is said to be "yawning"

YEARLING: a colt or filly that is a year old

PART 3

Horses of Today

From A-merican Saddle Horse to Z-ebra

There are many different breeds of horses. When a horse is said to belong to one breed, this does not mean that all his ancestors in the past were of that same breed. Some of the best breeds came into being because men purposely mated horses of one kind to mares of another, in order to produce a particular type of colt for which they had a particular need. A certain kind of mother might give her foal grace and speed, while another kind of father might give him strength and endurance. This kind of mating—over many generations—has produced most of the breeds known today.

A purebred horse is one whose mother and father were of the same breed. Many people make the mistake of calling such a horse a "thoroughbred." It is not correct to use this word in describing any other kind of purebred horse or animal—except a horse that really belongs to the Thoroughbred breed.

A crossbred horse is one whose mother and father were

of different breeds. Almost all farm horses used in America today are crossbreds, since few farmers can afford to buy purebred horses. Sometimes they prefer crossbreds to purebreds because such horses can do many different kinds of work.

All the distinct breeds of horses known today started in one of three main groups: the heavy draft, the tough and shaggy or the slender and rapid.

In the heavy draft group are the breeds that were used at first as knights' horses, then later came to be the work horses of the world—the pullers of wagons and coaches, the haulers of plows and fire engines. The tough and shaggy group contains the oldest and the smallest breeds in the world—the wild horses of Asia and the Shetland pony. And the slender and rapid group produces the glamorous breeds such as the Arabian, the Thoroughbred and the American quarter horse.

HEAVY DRAFT BREEDS

Belgian

Long ago there were three kinds of European horses: the black, which was large and muscular . . . the white, which was easy to manage and intelligent . . . and the bay, which was fast and strong. In these ancient times the land where the city of Brussels, Belgium, now stands was nothing but a huge pasture. The Germans called this pasture *Broisel*. They gave it this name because enormous herds of horses lived and raised their families there.

This is how the city of Brussels got its name. And from

38

the horses that lived there and were mated with the European black, white and bay horses came the draft horse breed known as the Belgian.

These were massive horses that served as chargers for medieval knights. They had to be big and husky in order to carry knights in their heavy suits of armor. Later on, merchants used these powerful animals to pull the wagons that held their wares. This is the only horse that is bred in any numbers in Belgium today, and there is probably some Belgian blood in almost every heavy draft breed in England.

As early as 1546 the English had a saying, "The gray mare will prove the better horse." In those days, people preferred the great gray horses of Belgium to pull their coaches.

The Belgians, together with the Shires, are the heaviest horses of the draft breeds. They stand about sixteen hands high, or five feet four inches. (A "hand" is four inches. The height of a horse is measured from the ground up to the tallest part of his withers.) They weigh around two thousand pounds and are bay, chestnut, roan and sometimes gray or black. They are stocky, with strong muscles and deep chests. Their legs are rather short and thick. Their gait is heavy because of their great weight.

Belgians usually have a calm, obedient disposition, making them easy to feed and care for. First brought to this country in the 1880's, their strength, willingness to work—and the low cost of caring for them—have made them valuable helpers on farms. The Belgian is the second most popular purebred draft horse used by American farmers.

The Clydesdale does most of the draft work in Scotland

Clydesdale

The Clydesdale breed was named after the river Clyde in Scotland, where it originated. This is the breed that still does most of the draft work in that country. It was first brought to North America by Scottish settlers in Canada.

The Clydesdale is probably a descendant of the chargers used by knights in their tournaments—the offspring of heavy Flemish horses and English draft mares. He is smaller than the Belgian, Percheron or Shire because animals that come from hilly lands, like the Scottish Highlands, are usually smaller than those that come from flat countries. The Clydesdale seldom stands taller than

40

sixteen hands and weighs under a ton. His body is much narrower than other draft horse breeds.

Although not too large, he is handsome. He wears shaggy tufts of hair, called feathers, on the backs of his legs below the knees. He always has white stockings and white on his face, while his coat is usually brown or bay, sometimes black, gray or chestnut. His gaits are more spirited than those of other large, but sluggish, horses. The Clydesdale moves proudly and briskly, lifting his feet well off the ground. This is why he is said to be the most refined breed of draft horse.

In days when horses were widely used in cities, the Clydesdale was popular because of his good looks, power and quick, high-stepping gaits. Nowadays, looks aren't as important in a work horse, so he isn't as popular as he used to be. People who still use draft horses object to the labor of keeping his long-haired legs clean. But in the Middle West, where a good draft horse is appreciated as much for his appearance as for his working ability, the Clydesdale is still widely used and liked.

Percheron

The Percheron is the breed of horse believed to have been ridden by French knights on their crusades. Joan of Arc rode one in the famous battles she led.

Named after a district in France called Le Perche, these horses were rediscovered back in the days when the French badly needed strong horses to pull their stage-coaches over very rough roads. They were first brought to America in the early 1800's and were later used in the Civil War to haul cannon and wagons. Since then they

41

Percherons are the most popular draft horse in the United States, which leads in raising them

have become the most popular draft horse in the country. There are more purebred Percherons here than all other draft breeds added together, and the United States has became the leading country of the world in raising and exporting this breed.

The Percheon earned his wide popularity because of the smart way he moves—and for his great strength and endurance. He stands about sixteen and a half hands (5′6″) and weighs more than a ton. Ninety per cent of all Percherons are now gray or black, although they were originally white. When they were still pulling coaches across France, however, it was too much trouble for stableboys to keep white horses clean—what with all the mud. So coach owners began to demand darker horses, while breeders tried to get only gray or black Percherons by not mating any white ones at all.

Farmers in the Middle West especially like this breed. The fearfully hot summers there are very hard on horses. Farmers claim that of all draft breeds, only the Percheron can stand this heat and yet keep right on working. They also like them because they move quickly and can turn in a small space, in spite of their size. At all midwestern fairs Percherons are among the prize exhibits. They are the horses in the famous painting by Rosa Bonheur called "The Horse Fair."

Shire

The Shire is the largest-known horse in the world. He stands about seventeen hands high (5'8"), often weighing as much as twenty-four hundred pounds. This great size was the result of a law that Henry VIII of England made. He ordered that all horses smaller than fifteen hands be destroyed because they were eating up a lot of England's limited pasture lands without doing enough hard work in return. Since he had only large parents for many generations, this enormous horse gradually developed into a distinct breed. The Shire is the work horse of England today.

His great size is the most unusual thing about a Shire's looks. He resembles a Clydesdale because he, too, wears white markings on legs and face, and has the same feathers on his feet and hocks. But the Shire is awkward. He moves ponderously, with none of the quick, smart step of the Clydesdale. And although the Shire is one of the very oldest purebred draft horses, he is also the one

Jack London, the famous writer, loved his blue-ribbon Shire like a friend

who seems to hate to work the most! Maybe this is because it is hard for him to carry around so much fat and muscle.

In fact, although the Shire does farm and pulling work, he doesn't show much enthusiasm for anything—except eating. This may be the reason that his popularity in America, ever since he was first imported in 1853, has been based more on the value of mating him with other faster, smaller and more alert mares than on the work he does. The colts that come from such a mating often grow up to be big, strong horses, but they have more "git-up-and-git" than their purebred papa. Every kind of horse has its admirers, however. Jack London, the famous writer, owned a blue-ribbon Shire stallion that he loved like a real friend.

Suffolk

Most draft horses can be used for all types of heavy work, whether pulling a city wagon or hauling a plow. But the Suffolk is strictly a country breed. It got its name from the farming county of Suffolk, England, where it originated.

Around 1770, English gentlemen-farmers used to stage tug-of-war exhibits with these horses. Fifteen Suffolks in a team pulled against the same number of horses in another team. Prizes were given to the team that out-pulled the other.

The Suffolk is a short-bodied horse that is almost always chestnut colored. A good Suffolk should not have white feet or feathers on his legs. He is a neat, clean-looking animal, easy to keep well groomed. He works for long hours, eats comparatively little and has a good disposition. He is one of the best farm horses there is. But because he should not be used for pulling really heavy wagons, American farmers prefer Percherons or Belgians which can both plow and pull. There are very few purebred Suffolks in this country. Today they are most commonly used in England.

TOUGH AND SHAGGY BREEDS

Wild Horses of Asia

The only truly wild horses of the world—except the zebra—are the tarpans that roam the steppes of Mongolia. They were discovered by a Russian explorer named Przhevalski. Sometimes these Asiatic wild horses are called Przhevalskis, in honor of the man who first found them in recent times.

Tarpans are smaller than tame horses. They have slender legs, large heads and rather big ears. Their mane stands up like a short, stiff brush from between their ears down to their shoulder blades. They are usually mouse, dun or tan colored. In the winter their shaggy coat grows quite long and thick—to protect them from the cold. It feels almost like a bear's coat.

Small bands of these wild horses, each band commanded by a leader-stallion, wander about the country near the borders of China. Like other wild animals they can smell human beings when they are still very far away. This makes them hard to catch, for as soon as they scent a person they run as fast as they can. The grown-up horses are impossible to tame even when they are captured. Colts can be tamed if they are caught when very young, but this hasn't been done often enough to make them of any real use to man.

Norwegian Dun

Some scientists believe the Norwegian Dun to be one of the first true breeds of all horses. This tough little animal has lived for countless years in the cold countries of Scandinavia. He is so sure footed that he makes an excellent mountain horse for people who have to ride long distances over hilly, rocky country.

The most striking thing about the Norwegian Dun's appearance is the color of his coat, from which he gets his name. Dun is a color ranging from a cream shade to

46

a dull brown. Because this is also the most common coat color of the tarpans, it is thought that the Norwegian Dun is related to them. He also has a dark stripe down the length of his spine and on his legs. Occasionally he may have stripes on his face, but this is rare. He has a pretty, clean-lined head, with bright eyes and alert, sharp little ears. He is very strong and brave for his rather small size. With his long, full tail and mane, he looks somewhat like a large pony.

He is a trotting horse, popular in his own northern countries. Norwegian Dun mares have also been exported to England to be bred with the famous Norfolk trotters there.

Shetland Pony

The breed perhaps best known and best loved by children is the Shetland pony. He is also the smallest member of the horse family. Sometimes he weighs only two hundred and seventy-five pounds, while the smallest Shetland on record stood only twenty-six inches high.

It is always good to call things by their correct names, so this is perhaps the place to explain just what a pony is. A pony is not a baby horse. A baby horse is first called a foal. A male foal is called a colt when he grows older, while a female foal becomes a filly. A baby horse is never properly called a pony, because a pony is a real, grown-up horse.

It *is* a horse, however, that stands no higher than fourteen hands (fifty-six inches). Any horse of any breed that is this size is a pony. A polo pony, for example, is still

47

The Shetland pony is a favorite with children

called a pony long after he has become a grandfather. Age has nothing to do with whether or not a horse is a pony. It all depends on his size.

The Shetland pony came originally from the Shetland Islands off the northern coast of Scotland. Not many people live on these islands because they are so barren that it is hard to raise food there. Perhaps the sparse vegetation of this hilly country was the reason why Shetland ponies stayed so small. They had to learn to thrive by eating almost anything that grows. Even today a Shetland does not have to eat any more than a goat does, in order to be healthy. He is usually spoiled, however, because he is such a lovable pet that his owners feed him too much. This makes him fat and is not good for him. It is really better for a Shetland to lead the rather rough life his ancestors did in Scotland.

Shetlands have been pets of man for a long time. On their rugged islands they slept in a family's poor hut and shared what food they had during the winter. This was not only because the pony was a good-natured little plaything, though. He was also useful. He was really a small draft horse—and has well earned the reputation of being able to pull or carry as many pounds of weight for his size as any larger horse.

The Scottish islanders used him to carry loads of peat, which is their kind of firewood. In England and Wales, Shetlands were used in the coal mines, their tiny size permitting them to pull loaded coal carts through low, narrow tunnels in the earth. One has been known to haul as much as 1000 pounds of coal in a single day's work. In 1950 some 17,440 such small horses, called pit ponies, were used underground in English mines.

Shetlands also have such strong backs that they can carry a grown man for a long distance. They can work in any kind of weather and they need very little special food. When not working they graze on the hills, eating whatever they can find. In winter their coat grows long and shaggy, but in summer it is short and smooth. They sometimes live to be thirty or forty years old. One Shetland was said to be a hundred years old, but this cannot be proved.

A Shetland pony is usually bay, brown or black, but American children seem to prefer those with a piebald or a black-and-white coat. Whatever his color he has a long, flowing tail and mane, with a graceful foretop falling between his bright eyes. His body is blocky, with short legs and back and rather large bones. Although he is pretty, sure-footed and has a kind disposition, the Shetland is not a very good riding horse. After a girl or boy has learned to ride a little, he should graduate to a better-gaited kind of pony or to a small saddle horse.

Shetlands are thought to be more intelligent than horses. This may be true because their ancestors for generations led such hard lives they had to learn how to take care of themselves almost all alone. Perhaps they passed on their quick wits to the little lovable Shetland pony of today.

SLENDER AND RAPID BREEDS

American Saddle Horse

One of the best-known breeds in the slender and rapid group is the American saddle horse. The United States has every right to be proud of this particular contribution to fine horseflesh.

This breed began in Kentucky long ago. In the days when people owned large plantations, before there were automobiles, the plantation owner used to inspect his property—or take long trips—on horseback. The weather was usually warm, so this southern gentleman wanted to ride as comfortably as he could, using as little physical exertion as possible. He thought long stirrups were easier on his legs—and he didn't like to rise to a trot in the English style. What he needed was a gentle, easygoing horse that would amble many miles without getting tired and without tiring the rider.

*The handsome American saddle horse is sometimes called
"the peacock of the horse world"*

Certain Kentuckians noticed that some rather plain mares, which had been brought to their state from Virginia and Tennessee, had a pleasant gait called a running walk. The plantation owners preferred such a gait to the trot or canter which were more popular up north. They began to select the mares with the best gait and mate them to the Thoroughbred horses with the best looks, endurance and spirit. In this way they soon had pretty, lively, easy-to-ride colts. As these grew up and had colts of their own, the American saddle horse breed was started.

This breed has since been so carefully raised and trained that it is one of the best of all breeds for people who want to ride just for pleasure. The American saddle horse is such a handsome animal and moves with such a smart rhythm that he has been called the "peacock of the horse world."

He wins many prizes at horse shows. If he is exhibited in a three-gaited class he shows his style first in a walk, then in a trot and finally in a canter. If he is a five-gaited horse his rider shows him in a walk, then a running walk, which is a faster walk and has four distinct hoofbeats. Next comes a trot, a still faster gait that is slightly up-and-down, the opposite front and back legs moving at the same time. Then follows a rack, a swift, easy gait between the speed of a trot and a canter, where each foot comes down separately—and finally a canter, a moderate gallop with a rocking horse motion, where both front feet come up at once with a spring. This gait used to be called the Canterbury gallop, after the town in England. It was a gentle gait such as was supposed to have been used by pilgrims riding to Canterbury.

The American saddle horse is medium sized, about fifteen hands high (five feet) and weighs around a thousand pounds. He is smart looking, with an arched neck and a proud stance. He is probably the horse that is most widely bred in the United States. Part of his great popularity is due to his peaceable nature, which makes him safe for children to ride.

Early Care and Training of a Saddle Horse

When a foal is born his eyes are open and he wears a rather rough coat of hair. He staggers right up on his long, knobby, shaky legs. He may even take a few steps before he lies down beside his mother. Within an hour or two, however, he stands up again and begins to nurse. Good horse trainers say that a foal should be handled and talked to by people before he is twenty-four hours old. This is to give him confidence in men, so he won't grow up either to fear or be shy of them.

By the time the foal is three days old he is about the same age as a one-year-old human baby. He gets his first teeth when he is only two weeks old, his full set of milk teeth by six months and his permanent set of big teeth by the time he is five years old. (Looking at a horse's teeth, if you know what to look for, has long been known to be the surest way of telling his age. As early as 1510 the great French writer Rabelais wrote, "Look a gift horse in the mouth." Most people today misquote this saying as *"Don't* look a gift horse in the mouth." This means that a present might prove to be disappointing if it is studied too carefully.)

Like a human baby a foal needs lots of rest during his

A very young foal's only food is his mother's milk

early weeks. He and his mother are given plenty of fresh water to drink and a block of salt to lick. But his only food is his mother's milk until he is two months old. Then he begins to eat grass, although he continues to drink milk until six months old.

It's hard for a colt to reach the grass at first, because his legs are long and unsteady, while his neck is still short. He has to spread his front feet wide apart in order to get his nose down to the ground. He also has to learn how to nibble so his lips will hold the grass firm while his front teeth bite it off. But soon he is managing very well as he gains strength by running around the paddock with his mother.

When he reaches his six-month birthday he becomes a weanling. Then he is taken away from his dam and put into a separate paddock with other weanlings. From then on, he is entirely on his own. In a surprisingly short time he has learned how to take care of himself.

While still a weanling he gets his first shoes. This experience makes him a little nervous, but he relaxes when he discovers it doesn't hurt. First, his hoof is filed smooth so the shoe will fit it. Then the blacksmith shapes soft, red-hot iron into a shoe by beating it with a hammer on his anvil until it's just the right size. When the hot iron takes the correct shape, the blacksmith cools and hardens it by plunging it into a bucketful of cold water. Then he fastens the new shoe to the colt's hoof with nails. Since the hoof is just a big, overgrown toenail, remember, this does not hurt at all.

Even before he's a year old the colt gets lessons in how to stand gracefully. Long reins are attached to his bridle, then the trainer stands before him holding the reins in one hand. In the other hand he holds a large wooden rattle. When he shakes the rattle the colt raises his head high in surprise at the sudden, funny noise. This gets his head into a good position and he soon learns to hold it that way.

When he reaches his first birthday he becomes a yearling. And when he is about two years old he is put under a saddle. For a while the trainer simply places a saddle on his back and lets him wear it until he gets used to the feel of it. When he seems calm and quite accustomed to the strange thing on his back, the trainer mounts him for the first time. If his teaching has been slow and patient, kind and understanding, it shouldn't be long before the young riding horse can then be trained to perfect the gaits he will use for the rest of his life.

Arabian

The beautiful and romantic Arabian horse has been so famous for so many years that it would take a whole book to tell all there is to tell about him. He is thought to be one of the oldest pure breeds—and almost every lightweight horse in America is believed to have some Arabian blood in his veins.

No one knows exactly where the Arabian horse first came from. It is strange that such a magnificent breed should have developed in a land where horses were never as common as they were in other parts of Asia. Actually, the camel, not the horse, is the national animal of Arabia. Even as late as 700 A.D., when horses were familiar creatures in many other countries, there were very few of them in Arabia.

This much *is* known, however, about the origin of the Arabian horse. After the civilizations of Assyria and Egypt had fallen, a group of horsemen called Bedouins invaded the desert land, bringing horses from Egypt, Persia or the southern coast of the Mediterranean Sea— no one knows exactly where. This lonely desert warrior depended on his horse for his very life. Since he was an invader, he needed some special advantage over the Arabians to prevent them from killing him or driving him out of their country. The one advantage he had was the speed of his horse. That's why the Bedouin bred his horses very carefully. He wrote a code of rules about their sale and breeding that is still followed. He kept accurate records of their ancestry—and he often fed them camel's milk, instead of water, to give them strength. He raised and trained his horses almost more intelligently than he did his children!

An Arabian horse is very devoted to his master

Man had been using horses only as tools to fight his wars, or pull his carts, for countless years before the Arabian horse. Now, because the Bedouin's life was so lonely and dangerous that he needed a reliable friend, the horse—for the first time in history—became man's companion instead of his slave.

Today the Bedouin's horse is still as much a part of his family as the dog is in America. He sleeps in the family tent and comes when called by name. The colt is given complete freedom to roam the open country, coming if his master calls him.

No Arabian horse that is brought up in Arabia knows

much about stables or stalls. And the Arabs wait until their colts are considerably older than American colts before they train them to a bridle. Because of his long, close relationship with man, and man's considerate care of him, the Arabian horse is said to be more devoted to his master than any other breed.

A recent story about an Arabian horse named Antez illustrates this:

The owner of a ranch out in the Far West was taking a ride on Antez one day. They went up into the hills. Suddenly, the saddle turned. The man fell right under his horse, one foot catching in a stirrup. Almost any other horse would have become panicky and bolted when this occurred. But not Antez. He stood perfectly still until others riding in the party came to the rescue. When his owner got untangled he remounted and they continued their ride as if nothing had happened.

Most horses are not noted for such intelligence, but perhaps this is because they have not been given the chance to be as close to man as Arabians have. A Bedouin's horse will pick up in his teeth and give his master a small article he may have dropped to the ground. He seems to be able to tell time, since he will indicate to his master the hour to get up and the hour to go to bed.

He stays by his master in any kind of trouble, rather than running away and leaving him in danger. And the Bedouin returns this devotion as his forefathers did. Although their life together is often hard, he will never commit the worst crime he can think of—the Bedouin will never sell his mare to a stranger.

The Arabian is a small horse—seldom over fifteen hands high—weighing around a thousand pounds. He has a beautiful, fine, wedge-shaped head, with wide-set eyes, small, pointed, very flexible ears and dark, flaring nostrils. His neck is arched, his tail and mane silken and flowing. He has such powerful lungs that the Arabs nicknamed him the "drinker of the winds." His stomach is small, his back short and sturdy, somewhat higher in the croup than the withers. His legs are slender, straight and strong, with broad hoofs that help him move over sand easily and quickly without sinking into it. Because he came from a desert country he has tremendous endurance. He can travel great distances in great heat, with little food or water.

The original decision as to which of his coat colors was the best was based on an old proverb of the Arabs: "Fleetest of horses is the chestnut; most enduring, the bay; most spirited, the black; most blessed, the one with a white forehead." Since black Arabians have always been rare, they were usually owned by Bedouin chiefs. White is a wonderful camouflage against the burning white of desert sand in blazing sunlight, so white horses were highly desirable. And since the chestnuts and browns proved to be speedy and have great endurance, these colors were also considered good. Today the solid black, white, bay, brown, gray or chestnut Arabians are the best. While a piebald, spotted or dappled horse may be *called* an Arabian, he is not really one.

The first Arabians were brought from North Africa to Spain—and from there to America in the sixteenth century. But their importance both here and in Europe is not based as much on the purebred horses themselves as on the wonderful qualities they have passed on to their colts when mated with other breeds. English horse breeders long ago crossed Arabian with English mares to get a colt that was larger and faster than the purebred Arabian— but without his endurance. This was the start of the racing horses now known as Thoroughbreds. Arabians have continued to contribute to the improvement of many other breeds. And in this way they still contribute to the work and pleasure of men.

Many famous people have owned and loved this particular breed, but perhaps the best known among them is Napoleon. He rode a beautiful white Arabian named Marengo in many of his campaigns. This horse was so beloved by the French that when he died his skin was stuffed. To this day he stands like a proud statue in a Paris museum.

Hackney

The Hackney breed originated in England around two hundred years ago. It was the result of mating Thoroughbred stallions to Norfolk mares. This horse very quickly became the favorite for pulling private carriages. Such a horse is called a heavy harness horse. The Hackney actually got his name from the type of carriage he most frequently drew. This same kind of carriage was used as a "horse taxi"—and today we sometimes call our taxicabs "hacks."

Hackneys—the horses, not the carriages!—can be as small as a pony or as tall as sixteen hands. But you can always distinguish a Hackney from other lightweight breeds because he has a thicker body and a wider chest and back, no matter what his height. Chestnut is his usual color, although he can also be bay, brown or red

Hackneys that pulled fancy carriages used to have their tails docked

roan. He sometimes has white stockings and a blaze of white on his face. His tail and mane are usually cut short when he is exhibited in a horse show, although this custom is disappearing.

It is not kind to dock a horse's tail because it is his only weapon against flies. Anyone who has been stung by a horsefly knows how painful that can be. Perhaps you have seen two horses standing, head to tail, in a meadow. This is so that each horse's tail will swish flies from the other horse's face—as well as from his own back and flanks.

Cruel as it was, however, all Hackneys that pulled fancy carriages used to have their tails docked because this style was considered more handsome. Usually driven in pairs, back in the days before automobiles, Hackneys made a pretty sight as they pranced along with their necks arched, their satin coats gleaming and their front feet lifted in high, graceful steps. People were as proud of their horses and carriages then as they are now of their brand-new automobiles. Whenever they wanted to make the best possible impression with a turnout, they used Hackney horses.

The breed is still popular for the harness class in horse shows and for riding. Although they are lovely to watch or to drive, their prancing gait and rather heavy bodies make them a little uncomfortable to ride. They often have headstrong dispositions, besides, which need careful control.

Today Hackneys are mainly owned by wealthy people who like to exhibit them in order to win blue ribbons or silver cups at horse shows. Since there is not much other demand for them, the breed may disappear in time. But even if it does, good Hackney blood will continue to flow in the veins of some of our other fine breeds and our greatest jumpers and hunters.

Morgan

The story goes that a singing teacher named Justin Morgan, of Vermont, went to Massachusetts some time in 1795 to collect a ten-dollar debt. When he got there the man who owed him the money couldn't pay him, but offered instead a small, stocky colt. Morgan liked the colt, so he accepted him. Together they walked back to Vermont, the teacher singing at inns along the way to pay for his room and board. When the colt grew into a fine young horse his master named him Justin Morgan, after

The Morgan is a breed that took its name from a single horse

himself. This horse became the great-great-great-grand-daddy of one of America's first truly distinct breeds of horses. It is the only breed known to have taken its name from a single horse. And Justin Morgan was the only horse ever to have started a breed all by himself!

He was a handsome animal, rather small and looking somewhat like an Arabian with his fine head and straight, slender legs. His coat was bay, but he had a black mane, tail and legs. He often won both trotting and running races. His ancestors were probably nondescript mares first brought here by New England settlers and later mated to English blood horses owned by rich farmers, English generals and American Revolutionary soldiers. Justin Morgan (the horse) lived to be twenty-nine years old and was the father of the many fine colts that continued this breed.

Today's Morgan horses are sometimes larger than Justin was, although the smaller ones are truer to type. They stand about fifteen hands and weigh around one thousand pounds. They are most often solid chestnut, brown, bay or black. Their eyes are bright, their ears small, while their necks have a nice natural arch. They were first used to clear the stony fields of Vermont, then as saddle, carriage and farm horses. They later became a preferred breed for many mounted police and for the Army.

They are still great favorites as saddle horses and for mountain trail riding, because they are strong, active and smart. For anyone who can afford to own only one light-weight horse, the Morgan is one of the best. The United States was so proud of this breed that the federal government maintained a farm in Vermont to raise, improve and perpetuate Morgans. The state of Vermont is carrying on this work, as are private breeders in this district.

The Morgan also gave many of his fine characteristics to other American breeds. During the days of early trotting and harness racing, Morgans proved to be the fastest horses. Sometime later, Morgan blood went into the breeding of the Standardbreds that are now considered to be the very finest of all trotting and pacing race horses.

Quarter Horse

Another breed that has good claim to be one of America's oldest is the quarter horse. In 1611, seventeen

64

English stallions and mares were brought to Virginia. They were mated to some of the descendants of the Spanish horses. Their colts had strong muscles, compact bodies and could run a short distance faster than any other breed. In 1656, races of a quarter of a mile in length were popular, and the American quarter running horse, as he was first called, got his name because he could run a quarter-mile race so fast.

This was really a racing breed that was developed even before the famous Thoroughbred breed in England. The quarter horse spread all over the United States because he was the speediest short-distance horse in the world at a time when short races were the most popular kind. After it became fashionable to run races of longer distances and Thoroughbreds were imported into this country for this purpose, the quarter horse became famous in the Southwest.

Some people say he has proved to be the greatest cow horse of all time. He is used on our ranches and as a race horse, and he is often bred to mustangs to get colts that are supposed to be even *better* cow horses!

The quarter horse stands between fourteen and fifteen hands (4'8" and 5') and weighs between one thousand and twelve hundred pounds. His muzzle is short and his eyes are big and set wide apart. His ears are the small kind called fox ears, while his nostrils are large. He has a short back and sloping shoulders, with powerful muscles and legs. He has earned his reputation as a cow pony because of his physical equipment, his good disposition and his great speed over short distances.

Recently, he has become almost equally popular as a saddle horse. He is intelligent, easy to train and handle,

The quarter horse is a wonderful cow pony

with a dependable nature that makes him safe for women and children to ride. Since he was bred to live in open country with cattle, he needs little care or special food. He is as much at home on an acre of pasture as he is on the largest range. Some of the top polo ponies in the country have been quarter horses.

Standardbred

The Standardbred has sometimes been called the American trotting horse. But since this is the breed that also produces pacers as well as trotters, Standardbred is the preferred name.

A trotting horse that races is one who trots very fast with the *left* foot on the front moving at the same time as the *right* foot in the back, and vice versa.

He pulls a driver who rides in a tiny, light carriage called a sulky. The sulky holds only one person, has two bright, shining wheels like bicycle wheels—and not much more! (It gets its name because, since only one person could ride in it, that person might be called "sulky" and want to be left alone.) A trotter has been trained not to break from the gait of a trot in his race, no matter how fast he goes.

A pacing horse that races is one who takes long, running steps with the *left* foot in the front moving at the same time as the *left* foot in the back, and vice versa. He pulls the same kind of sulky as the trotting horse, and he, too, has been trained never to break from his gait into a canter or a gallop. Pacers race against other pacers, trotters against trotters. Both kinds of horses are used in the particular sport called harness racing.

The Standardbred is the breed that has produced the greatest trotters and pacers. Some Europeans think they are America's most valuable contribution to horse breeding. The Standardbred began with a mixture of Hackney, Thoroughbred and Morgan blood—in New England around the end of the eighteenth century. Raising this kind of horse on a large scale started before the Civil War on farms around the towns of Goshen and Chester in New York State.

The great-grandfather of most present-day trotters was a dark bay stallion named Hambletonian. His name was

The Standardbred has produced some of the world's finest trotters and pacers

given to one of the most important of all trotting races, the Hambletonian. This race is run every year on the track at Goshen, and has the richest prizes of any harness race in the world.

A good Standardbred is from fifteen and a half to sixteen hands high and weighs from one thousand to twelve hundred pounds. He often has a back that is longer than his height, and stands higher at the croup than at the withers. His ears, head and bones are larger and coarser than a Thoroughbred's. He can be almost any horse color. Before the time of automobiles he used to be a popular buggy horse or light farm horse, as well as a racer. His disposition is trustworthy because he is not so fiery tempered as a Thoroughbred. He makes a good saddle horse.

But the Standardbred made his reputation mainly as a

trotter or pacer. He should keep that reputation as long as there are harness races in any country.

Tennessee Walking Horse

The Tennessee walking horse is another purely American breed, but one that is rather new. It was originally called the Plantation walking horse and was recognized as a distinct breed only some one hundred years ago. Like the American saddle horse of Kentucky, he was first used by plantation owners in Tennessee to ride around their many acres of property. These men liked him because of his comfortable natural gaits and his endurance.

He was developed from a mixture of Thoroughbred, Standardbred, Morgan and American saddle horse breeds, getting many good qualities from each. He was originally raised for three purposes—riding, pulling carriages and for light farm work. Today he is used most often as a saddle horse for pleasure riding.

The Tennessee walking horse is noted for his three natural gaits—the flat-footed walk, the running walk and the canter. All three are very smooth and pleasant. The flat-footed walk is a slow gait, like any walk, where opposite front and back feet move at the same time. The horse sort of shuffles his feet along the ground so that his body bounces very little. But it was the running walk that really made this breed famous. This is a gait that a horse must be born with—it cannot be taught to him by man.

In the running walk the legs move the same as in the flat-footed walk, but at a greater speed. Gradually, the stride becomes so long that the hind foot actually steps over the track left by the front foot. This gives a gliding motion so pleasant that the rider can continue at this pace for a long time without getting tired. The running walk is almost as fast as a trot, but it does not have the trot's jolting, up-and-down motion. During this gait the Tennessee walking horse nods his head in time to his steps, often swinging his ears and snapping his teeth in his own enjoyment.

The canter is a fast, springing gait like a refined gallop. The Tennessee walking horse has been called "Nature's rocking chair" because his canter is very rhythmic, smooth and easy to ride.

He stands about fifteen and a half hands and weighs between one thousand and twelve hundred pounds. Although his lines are fine, he has great stamina. He can be sorrel, chestnut, black, roan, white bay, gray or brown. He sometimes has white feet and a white blaze or star on his head. His tail is long and flowing, and when he is being exhibited in a horse show his mane is braided into tiny pigtails tied with ribbons. His head is neat, with pointed ears, large eyes and a tapered muzzle. He has a long neck set on strongly muscled sloping shoulders.

Besides being so pleasant to ride, he is hardy and therefore easy to raise. His disposition is never vicious. He is intelligent, simple to train—and has gentle manners that make him an ideal mount for women and children. People who live in Tennessee often hold what they call "ride-a-thons." Mounted on their Tennessee walking horses, whole families and their friends ride along quiet trails across the country.

The radio funnyman Arthur Godfrey recently bought

a Tennessee walking horse, while more and more horse shows are featuring exhibitions of this fine breed.

Thoroughbred

Thoroughbred is the name of a distinct breed of horses that race by galloping with jockeys on their backs over turf, which is grass, or track, which is earth. This breed started in England around 1670, when Charles II imported several Barb mares from North Africa to add to his racing stables.

Later, three Arabian stallions were brought to England. They were named Byerly Turk, Darley Arabian and Godolphin Arabian, and they became the great-great-great-granddaddies of all the true Thoroughbreds known today. Their offspring were mated to lightweight English mares who had shown that they could run very fast. What the English racing breeders wanted were horses of greater speed than the purebred Arabian had, but with the Arabian's famous endurance. By careful crossbreeding they eventually developed the Thoroughbred breed. It is one of the oldest man-made breeds, as distinguished from natural breeds like the Arabian and the Norwegian Dun. And today's Thoroughbred is the "glamour horse" of the world, because it is so well known for its racing and so skillfully bred and cared for.

A son of Darley Arabian was brought to Virginia in 1730, and many thousands of Thoroughbreds have since been imported into America. But the United States now raises its own Thoroughbreds, and some of the champion race horses of history have been American bred, like Man o' War, Citation, Whirlaway and many others. Americans

71

have also used Thoroughbreds to cross with other breeds to produce some of the very best American breeds.

Thoroughbreds stand between sixteen and seventeen hands (5′4″ and 5′8″) and weigh between one thousand to fourteen hundred pounds. They are usually dark in color—solid chestnut, bay, black or gray, with only small white stars or stockings. They are never piebald.

Since the main object in breeding them was to get speed, they have great, strong muscles, straight powerful legs—and deep chests so they can breathe well when running fast. They have an Arabian's small, pointed, alert ears and wide, bright eyes—and they hold their heads proudly. Hot-blooded animals, they seem to love to run—and win!—a race better than anything else. Because they usually represent an investment of a lot of money, they are exceptionally well groomed. This shows in their gleaming satin coats, their well-brushed flowing tails and manes and their high spirits.

The Thoroughbred will be one of the most popular breeds of horses as long as running races are one of the most popular sports. In addition to his own value, however, the Thoroughbred must also be thanked for the gifts of speed, looks and endurance that he has passed on to his colts of other breeds.

ALMOST BREEDS

Some of the best-known horses are those that do not belong to any one breed but are considered in a separate class for a special reason. Such horses are the hunter, the mustang, the polo pony, and the palomino.

The hunter is a type of horse that is especially adapted to the work (and fun) of carrying his rider across rough country during a fox hunt. He can jump ditches, fences, streams or brambles. He can run fast enough to keep up with the hounds that are trailing the fox.

Some of the best hunters are raised in Ireland. They are descendants of Irish Thoroughbreds crossed with Irish cart horses. (Most good hunters are thought to have some Thoroughbred blood.) The Irish hunters graze on grassland that is rich in limestone. This gives them the large, solid bones they need. America, too, produces good hunters, although fox hunting has never been as popular here as it is in England and Ireland.

Hunters are classified into three groups, depending on the weight of the rider they are expected to carry. A light-weight hunter carries anyone weighing from one hundred and thirty-five to one hundred and sixty-five pounds; a middleweight, from one hundred and sixty-five to one hundred and ninety pounds; a heavyweight, from one hundred and ninety pounds and over. They can be of any breed, as long as they can jump obstacles at least five feet high in an open field. And they must be strong, intelligent, quick—and have enough stamina to run to the very end of a hard, cross-country hunt.

Hunters' manes are sometimes hogged close to the neck, while their tails are usually either docked or bound up in a tight roll with bandages when hunting. This is to prevent possible spills caused when long hairs catch in briers or fence splinters. If such hairs are caught, this hurts the horse and often pulls him off balance. When a person owns a mount that likes to kick out at horses with his rear hoofs, he often ties a red ribbon on his hunter's tail to warn other riders to keep a safe distance.

Riding enthusiasts also use their best hunters for what is called point-to-point racing. This is a race from a starting point to a finish line—over many miles of open country. In such a race the horse has to jump the same kinds of obstacles as when hunting. It is a sport that demands quick thinking on the part of both horse and rider. This is the reason it is considered one of the best tests of true horsemanship.

Mustang

The mustang is a most exciting type of horse for any boy or girl who likes a rodeo, books about cowboys or western movies. This is one kind of horse cowboys ride, as well as the kind that supplies most of the broncos for rodeos.

A bronco is not a breed. It is a word that comes from the Spanish word meaning "wild." It is applied to a horse of any breed that refuses to be saddlebroken. Most broncos are mustangs, and there is a good reason for this.

Remember the Spanish horses that escaped from Cortes and De Soto? The Indians captured and tamed some of their descendants but not all. Others wandered around our Far West in small bands, almost completely wild. They "elected" their own leaders by staging tough fights between the two strongest stallions in the band. The one who used his teeth and hoofs the most skillfully won the fight and became the band's leader—until he grew old and lost his fight to a younger stallion.

74

Westerners say mustangs are natural-born cow ponies

When the cow hands of the early days of the Far West heard about these groups of semiwild horses, they hunted them down, captured them and trained them to work on the ranges. Those horses that refused to be tamed were the broncos, but by and large the tamed mustangs were natural-born cow horses.

Mustangs kept the cattle together on the long journeys up from the feeding ranges to the fattening pens— and then to the railroad, where they were shipped to city markets. Without the mustang our huge ranching industry might never have been developed. He was tough and strong. He found his own grass and water in the most barren land. He traveled over the roughest ground and swam the wildest streams, always keeping his eye on the cattle to see that they didn't scatter or run away. He really had what westerners call "cow sense."

Early scouts and explorers of our Far West also found mustangs useful as trail horses. The story is told of one scout who had been given a mustang by a chief of the Sioux Indians. When the men camped at night, sleeping on the ground, this scout let his horse loose to eat all the buffalo grass he wanted. After he was full, the horse sniffed each sleeping man until he found his master. Carefully lying down beside him, they kept each other warm until dawn. No enemy Indian could come near the camp without this mustang's giving the alarm.

The mustang is still used on our ranches. He is usually the bay, gray or dun colors of the original Spanish horses, but he may also be piebald or pinto. He is small, stocky and extremely sure footed. His mane and tail are long, his legs rather slender. While not a beautiful horse, he is one of the hardest of workers. In spite of a temper that is hard to control, our cowboys like him so much that they go to all the trouble of rounding up the bands of wild mustangs that continue to breed and live on their own in the West.

The cowboys first find the place where these horses are grazing. Then they study the lay of the land to decide which way the horses will run when they sense danger. If this is down a valley, the cowboys build a large wooden pen with an open mouth. They then place other cowboys along the sides of the valley to frighten the horses into the open mouth of the pen.

Next they ride quietly upwind toward the wild horses,

so the animals won't scent them. When they get behind the band they gallop toward them all of a sudden, terrifying the wild horses into a stampede. As they gallop wildly down the valley toward the trap, the cowboys on its edges drive them in the right direction. Finally the whole band of wild horses finds itself in the wooden pen. The cowboys slam the gate on them, and there they are—ready to be broken.

This work of rounding up wild mustangs, then breaking and training them, takes a lot of time and effort. But it is worth it to the cowboys in order to get such good cow ponies.

Polo Pony

Like the hunter, the polo pony can be of any breed. Thoroughbreds, Arabians and quarter horses are some of the many breeds that have produced good polo ponies.

It is not the breed that is important, however. It is the pony himself—his temperament and physical equipment. For polo ponies are made, not born. But before a man can make one his partner in this tough, rough-and-ready game of hockey-on-horseback, he must first pick a horse that has certain qualities.

A good potential polo pony should not be too tall or too heavy, because he must be able to turn on a dime. He should stand between fourteen and fifteen hands and weigh from nine hundred to eleven hundred pounds. He must love the game. He must be very strong, fast and alert. He must have great endurance to carry his rider up and down and across the field after the ball. He should have a deep chest, a short back and straight legs. He has to be in the best of health, with sound, powerful lungs. He should also be willing to get near other horses, even push them around when he has to.

Argentina and Texas now raise some of the world's best polo ponies. Both are cattle lands, for the special qualities needed in a good polo pony are also needed in a good cow pony. Just as a good cow horse keeps his eye on the cattle, so a good polo pony learns to keep his eye on the ball. Although few polo ponies ever become as famous as outstanding Thoroughbred race horses, they should really win the very highest honors of all the sporting horses. Perhaps more is required of them than of any other kind of horse that man uses exclusively for his pleasure.

Palomino

Palomino is the name given to a horse of any breed that has a coat of a special color—the color of a golden coin. He usually has a white mane and tail. There can be white on a palomino's face, and he can have white stockings below his hocks, but no stripes or piebald markings on his body. His skin and nose must be dark, and he has dark, hazel or black eyes.

This name has been given to horses of such coloring for only a very short time. Long ago, some Morgans, American saddle horses, Tennessee walking horses or quarter horses were described as having golden coats with flaxen manes. They were considered unusual and extremely beautiful. Most of today's palominos are the descendants of the original Spanish horses of that color, crossed with our western cow ponies and other breeds.

The palomino is not a distinct breed, but it is expected to become one within a few more years. Horse breeders are working toward this end by mating palominos to other breeds of the same coloring. Eventually, they hope to have enough true palominos to be able to mate them only with each other and produce palomino colts. When this happens, another man-made breed of horses will have been created.

Anyone who has ever seen a palomino in a circus, rodeo, horse show, parade—or working on a ranch—will agree that this is one of the most beautiful of all animals. In addition to his striking color, a good palomino should also have strong feet and legs, and a body that conforms to the type of work he is supposed to do.

Since the palomino still comes from many different breeds, he falls into three main classes:

1. the stock horse, which does the same cow work on a ranch as the mustang or quarter horse

2. the pleasure horse, which is a saddle horse of pleasant gait, like the American saddle horse

3. the parade horse, which is used mostly for display parades in rodeos and horse shows, and resembles the Arabian or Thoroughbred

In judging palominos at shows or state fairs, the same standards are applied as to any breed that competes as a jumper, saddle horse or stock horse. But special emphasis is placed on the color of these horses. A palomino of excellent coloring will rate a higher place than a palomino of inferior coloring, even if the latter has performed better. The Palomino Parade is becoming one of the most popular events at fairs and shows. It is indeed something to see! Long flaxen manes and tails flowing, golden coats shining, dark eyes flashing, they walk or trot proudly around and around the ring. They are decked out in gorgeous silver-studded saddles and bridles worth many hundreds of dollars, while their riders wear bright silk costumes, usually of a Spanish or Mexican style.

The palomino should be considered a worthy product of America, if only for his beauty. But when it is understood that palomino stock or saddle horses also work as well as any other breed, it is clear why they are so popular.

ALMOST HORSES

There are certain animals that one would never think of as belonging to the horse family. Such animals might be called "almost horses," although the donkey, the mule and the zebra are all true members of the horse family.

Donkey

Donkey is the widespread nickname of the ass or burro. The ass belongs to an ancient and honorable breed that is believed to have descended from the wild asses of North Africa. He was used as a saddle and draft animal while the horse was still only pulling chariots. Although the horse is seldom mentioned in the Bible, the donkey is written about as if he were the common animal of the Holy Land. He was later used for riding, carrying packs and pulling carts in Spain. Probably because a donkey thrives in mountainous lands, Spanish burros became famous throughout Europe for their ability to do a lot of work on a small amount of food.

One early historian writes about performing donkeys in the sixteenth century who did such tricks as dancing and "playing dead." Another tells of a remarkable ass named Valiant.

Valiant was sold by a merchant in Gibraltar and then put on a ship to be sent to his new master. Some distance out at sea the ship began to sink in a violent storm. The ass was thrown overboard in the hope that he might swim ashore. But this seemed impossible, because the waves were terribly high. A few days later, however, when the guards unlocked the city gates of Gibraltar, Valiant trotted in and went right to the merchant's stable. He had not only swum ashore, but he had found his way across some two hundred miles of unfamiliar mountainous country—back to his own stall!

It is good to remember such examples of intelligence when you hear people speak of a stupid donkey. Donkeys have worked so hard and faithfully for so many generations—often beaten and mistreated—that they haven't had much opportunity to display the very real intelligence they possess.

The donkey is better equipped than the horse for carrying loads, because his shoulders are lower than his croup. This helps to hold a pack on his back. He eats coarser food and needs less water than a horse. Probably because he was originally raised in hot climates where it was hard to get water, he just wets his lips when he drinks. He has a tough skin, and he loves to roll in dry dirt to scratch his hide. Although most of the donkeys we know are dark in color, those that live in Egypt and India are light gray or sometimes even white. Their legs are short, their backs strong—and of course they are all noted for their long ears.

The work they do is well known, but it is not so commonly realized that more children have burros for pets than Shetlands. They have such a patient, gentle personality that it is a shame they are not better treated by their owners—and better appreciated by the rest of the world for all the labor they have done for so many hundreds of years.

Mule

Another "almost horse" is the mule. Properly speaking, the mule is not a breed. No book on the horse would be complete, however, without mentioning this hard-working friend of man.

A mule is a hybrid. This means that every mule has a horse—called a mare—for a mother, and a donkey—called a jackass—for a father. Since mules cannot have baby mules of their own, they will never become a distinct breed. And since a mule's only forebears are his donkey daddy and his mare mother, he has no ancestors, in the real sense of the word. Each mule is a separate animal, with no past and no future.

Although many silly stories have been spread about the poor mule, he was not always looked down upon. He was used for generations in the Near East to carry packs and turn water wheels. People rode on muleback in caravans over the deserts. In France, Spain and Italy, teams of mules decked in fine harness pulled royal carriages. And none other than George Washington himself took a

The little donkey and the strong mule are both hard-working friends of man

great interest in raising the first American mules. In 1786 he advertised in a Philadelphia newspaper that he had a splendid jackass, named Royal Gift, which had just been given to him by the King of Spain. Washington instructed those who wanted to mate their mares with this fine animal to get in touch with him by letter at Mount Vernon.

The mule played an important role in war, both as saddle and pack animal. And in the diary of a man who traveled by ox team from Missouri to California in the Gold Rush days, we read: "September 11, 1849. One hundred and forty miles east of Sacramento. We passed a government mule-train from San Francisco. They are on pack mules. The train consists of one hundred and twenty mules and thirty-two men. They are exploring a route of a railroad across the Sierra Nevada Mountains." This was the railroad that later became the great Union Pacific line which connected the Middle West with California. It shows how the mule helped build this country.

Today the lowly mule is the mascot of the West Point Military Academy's football team.

In looks, the mule resembles the horse, except for his long ears, rather hairless tail and the braying voice which he inherits from his donkey father. A good mule has a compact body, with a broad chest and short back. His coat is soft and silky, usually black, brown, bay or gray. Mules with spotted coats are called pintos by the Mexicans and Chickasaws by our Negroes in the South. Solid colors are believed to mean stronger animals, however.

Over half of the mules used in America today are in the southern states, where they plow fields and carry the picked cotton to market. While they do the same work as a horse, they don't eat as much—are more sure footed, less nervous, less irritable. Besides, they live longer. A mule has often been called stubborn. Some people think this may well be because he is more intelligent than a horse. Unlike a horse, which will do on command what he has been trained to do, a mule likes to figure things out for himself. Because he isn't as fiery or impatient as a horse, he usually takes his time in deciding what is best to do. But with gentle and understanding treatment— instead of a cruel whip and harsh words—the faithful, hard-working mule can be persuaded to do anything.

Zebra

Together with the tarpans, the zebras are the only truly wild horses in the world today. On the African continent,

In ancient days, the zebra was called the "horse tiger"

defenseless animals need camouflage to protect themselves from the many large, savage, meat-eating animals that live there. So gradually, after hundreds of years, the African wild horse developed a striped coat which resembled the shadows cast on the ground by sunlight—or moonlight shining through jungle trees. This disguise made it hard for lions, tigers or men to see and kill the zebra. The very name "zebra" comes from an Abyssinian word that means "of a black-and-white stripe." In ancient days the zebra was also called the "horse tiger."

Like tarpans and American wild horses of the West, zebras travel in small groups and elect their own leader-stallion. Unlike other horses, however, the zebra also welcomes the company of certain other animals. Hunters have often seen the zebra grazing with ostriches and gnus.

There is a good reason for this odd companionship. The only weapon the zebra, ostrich and gnu have against ferocious enemies is their speedy legs. Consequently, these three animal friends make up a small mutual-aid society. The ostrich, with his long neck and exceedingly sharp eyes, keeps watch over the heads of the zebra and the gnu, warning them of danger. The gnu, with his very sharp ears, can hear a hidden enemy that the ostrich might fail to see. While the zebra, which has the sharpest sense of smell of them all, can warn the others when he scents a silent, hidden foe that they could neither see nor hear. Such a close relationship among animals of different species is so rare that it makes this combination a real curiosity.

The zebra isn't of any great use to modern man. He has been hunted as food by Africans, but he has never been much help in tilling the soil or pulling carts. Once in a while zebras have been broken to harness, but they do not work nearly as well as horses or mules.

PART 4

Horses at Work

WAR HORSES

One of the first ways in which man used his friend, the horse, was to help him fight his wars. For hundreds and hundreds of years the poor horse carried soldiers on his back, pulled heavy guns, dragged ammunition and food wagons, got himself wounded and killed—all for man.

Horses have been used in almost every American war. Nearly every history book has a copy of the famous painting that shows General Washington seated on his charger Nelson when he received Cornwallis' surrender at Yorktown. General Grant rode his horse Jack for three years in the Civil War, while the Confederate general, J. E. B. Stuart, was a noted cavalryman.

General Custer rode his famous mount Comanche in one of the last of the Indian wars. Comanche was an ugly, rough horse that had been captured by the Indians when wild, then sold to one of Custer's men. It was Comanche who was the only survivor of Custer's "last stand." His wounds were cared for until he was well, then he became

Horses have been used in almost every American war

the mascot of the Seventh Cavalry. Comanche lived in a special stall—and no one ever rode him again. He has often been called "America's most heroic horse."

All countries were still using cavalry in World War I. Little by little, however, most armies became completely mechanized. In World War II, only the famous fiery Cossack horses of the Russians saw much fighting.

Horses were owned mainly by knights and royalty for crusades and war—up to the end of the Middle Ages in Europe. But when commerce began to be as profitable to nations as wars, poorer people began to use horses, too. Merchants rode horseback, peddling their wares from village to village. Pack horses carried goods along roads that weren't much wider than footpaths. Blacksmith shops for horses' sore feet—and inns for tired, hungry riders—were opened along the most popular trails. Villages grew into towns and towns into cities, as their industries became bigger. Pack and trail horses started the roads over which the coach horses later established regular contact between cities and countries that wanted to trade with each other.

In America similar trading was carried on with the help of horses. Furthermore, horses really opened the way to the Far West. Daniel Boone broke the first trails westward when he led an expedition of families toward Kentucky. Everyone and everything in that expedition was carried on horseback. There was not a single wagon, for even the smallest cart could not make its way through the thick forests or over the rough land. Children rode in large baskets that were slung from each side of the saddle. Only cows, pigs and dogs followed on foot. Boone and his men on horseback later cut a narrow road into the heart of Kentucky. This made possible the very beginning of the great migration to the Far West. It could not have been successful without the sure-footed trail horses who carried the pioneers through the wilderness, or the pack horses who carried their food, bedding, clothing and ammunition.

Pack horses even served as ferryboats. When the pioneers came to streams that were too deep to wade, they blew up big skin bags. They tied these to the horse's tail to help him float, then placed people or goods on his back—and the horse swam the stream.

As more and more men wanted to move to the rich western farm lands, regular pack horse trains were formed. Miners, fur trappers, traders, and settlers traveled together on horseback, following trails that became more clearly marked with constant use. In the 1780's as many as fifty such trains—of ten or more horses each—passed through Pennsylvanian towns. When the new American government began to build roads they often followed these old trails, while covered wagons took the place of pack trains. But trail and pack horses still went along with the wagons for many, many years.

Trail and pack horses are still used in many parts of the world where travel by other means is difficult or impossible. Mountain explorers and surveyors for new engineering projects often ride horseback. People on vacation at dude ranches ride trail horses along mountain paths where no automobile can go.

Some eastern states hold regular yearly cross-country rides along trails. Not as rough as a steeplechase or as fast as point-to-point racing, special rules must be obeyed —and prizes are given to the horse who makes the best time. City folk who love horses, but don't get much chance to ride them, often take vacations in Vermont. There they can rent mounts and ride over some one thousand miles of quiet, beautiful bridle paths, sleeping at inns or farmhouses at night.

Even on the far-off island of Java, trail horses are used for sight-seers who wish to visit a certain extinct volcano. Because the days are so hot, the trip from the nearest town is made at night. Mounted on a small horse, you ride up steep, narrow paths, a bright moon stabbing silver light through the pine forests that surround you. At your pony's head walks a barefooted Indonesian boy who wears a sarong and a turban, a tin box slung by a strap across his brown shoulders.

For several hours the ponies plod surely and carefully up and over the hills, never stumbling in the dark. Then, just as dawn breaks, you stop at the edge of the forest. Spread out before you are the gray lava sands of the volcano's crater. The sun climbs over banks of rose and gold clouds. You get off your horse to enjoy the magnificent view. Then the boy opens the mysterious tin box and gives you your breakfast: an orange, a roll with butter and marmalade, topped off with coffee or milk from a Thermos. You eat while you watch the sun rise. Then you pat your pony's nose and thank him and the boy for bringing you safely to such an unusual sight.

CONESTOGA HORSES

Conestoga horses were not a special breed. They were heavy Pennsylvania draft horses that were too large to be practical for pack train trails or for riding in town. They got their name from the kind of wagons they pulled. The first covered wagons were called Conestoga wagons, after

Conestoga wagons were often called prairie schooners

the town in Pennsylvania where they were manufactured.

These wagons were about the largest horse-drawn vehicles ever known. Made of wood, they had rear wheels as high as a horse, and tall side walls. Wooden hoops arched across the wagon, holding heavy cloth that formed a roof. Rather like today's auto-trailers, they were rolling homes that had beds like a ship's bunks, some rough furniture, even enough room for the household pets! Probably because they looked like huge boats as they moved over the plains, they were often called prairie schooners.

The driver of a Conestoga wagon rode on the back of the left rear horse, holding the reins of the lead horses. Four or six horses pulled such wagons. One of the first jobs these wagons did was to carry commercial goods, like trucks do today. With a big sign painted on the canvas sides of the roof, reading PHILADELPHIA TO PITTSBURGH IN TWENTY DAYS, they made the trip that today takes about six hours in a fast car.

Conestogas were also organized into caravans of families that were moving ever farther west. All true Conestoga wagons were painted bright red with blue trimming, and had striped cloth for their roofs. The horses were

92

decked out with red cords and bells. Such a caravan of color made a pretty sight as it moved across the prairies.

Conestoga horses and wagons were not used as far as the Rockies. The covered wagons that made the dangerous journey beyond these mountains were much plainer —and were usually pulled by a yoke of oxen. Horses were ridden by scouts who went ahead to lead the way and warn of possible perils.

Canalboat Horses

After the Erie Canal was constructed, many other canals were dug in order to connect rivers, lakes and cities for trade among the eastern states. This was also how travel westward by canalboat began.

Such boats were long, round-bottomed barges with large rooms where all passengers slept at night and ate in the daytime. A rope was attached to the bow of the boat. This was connected to a single horse—or sometimes to a

Pulling a canalboat was one of the easiest jobs a horse could have

team of horses—that walked on a path bordering the canal. The horse, with a rider on his back, pulled the boat through the water.

This was perhaps one of the most enjoyable ways to travel that man ever invented, although it was rather slow. One glided quietly, comfortably and safely through green fields while he ate, slept or admired the scenery. There was also plenty of room to move around when one wanted exercise. Pulling the canalboat was also one of the easiest jobs a horse could have. Well fed and cared for, he kept walking at a steady gait of about two miles an hour along a fairly wide, even path. It was not very difficult to tow the boat through the calm water.

Some five thousand miles of these waterways connected the eastern states by the time the railroad began to take the place of this pleasant method of travel.

Coach Horses

There were few carriages of any kind in Shakespeare's England, since most people still rode horseback then. Some hackney coaches later appeared for hire, but they weren't used much. It wasn't until the eighteenth century that coaches—and therefore coach horses—really became important as a means of transportation.

Stagecoaches were the quickest method of traveling in those days. Four horses pulled a coach, to be replaced by four fresh horses when the coachman stopped at an inn to pick up or discharge passengers—and have a hot drink. The two front horses, called leaders, set the pace. The two rear horses were called wheelers. Although they, too,

The time of the coach horse was a romantic period

did their share of pulling when running ahead, wheelers were trained to act as brakes to prevent the coach from going too fast down a hill.

Since four strong horses hauling a carriage at high speed often turned corners too fast—or failed to stop a downhill rush in time, or simply got frightened and ran away—there were many accidents on the stagecoaches. Yet it was a romantic period of galloping hoofs, cracking whips, highwaymen—and interesting stops at country inns along the road. Many Englishmen hated to see the end of the stagecoach when steam engines began to be used. As one writer of the time said, "How lamentable that it should be put aside for that nasty, wheezin', crackin', puffin', gaspin', bustin' monster!"

Other countries also had their stagecoaches. The French used Percherons to pull theirs, and also developed a special breed of heavy, fast horses called the French

Coach. The Germans had their own breed, too, called the German Coach. And America had its stagecoaches from the very beginning of the republic.

American coaches of Colonial days were painted bright colors, with trimmings of gilt and pictures painted on the side panels. Nine to twelve people sat on three or four seats that were upholstered in silk. One of the first journeys of such a public coach in the colonies took place in 1772, between New York and Boston. Following the famous Boston Post Road, the trip took one week in the summer, nine or ten days in winter.

There was great competition among the different coach companies, so their drivers always raced each other at top speed for great distances over very rough roads. Such trips were hard on the horses, though, and they could not have been exactly comfortable for the passengers. During the winter, the coach wheels were replaced by runners so the horses could drag them through deep snow.

Later, the stagecoach lines divided their business by specializing in what they carried. One line took mail; another, passengers; a third, light freight, and so on. These lines had such colorful names as the June Bug Line, the Oyster Line and the Shake Gut Line!

One of the most famous of these lines was started after a railroad ran from the East to the Mississippi River. This was the Overland Stage Mail. At that time there were no railroads running from St. Louis, Missouri, to San Francisco, California. Nor were there any regular stagecoaches covering those twenty-eight hundred miles of barren country. After gold was discovered in California in 1849, however, Congress passed a bill authorizing such a line of stagecoaches. This filled a great demand for some quick, reliable way of transporting people, freight and mail from Missouri to the West Coast.

No roads ran through the Southwest Territory. There were constant dangers from holdups, breakdowns, unfriendly Indians and accidents far from any medical or mechanical help. The trip cost one hundred and fifty dollars per passenger. Everyone carried a rifle, a revolver, ammunition, warm clothing, blankets, soap and plenty of food that could be eaten without stopping. For the coaches stopped only long enough to change horses at stations some thirty to fifty miles apart. The passengers had to sleep sitting up and eat when they could. It was a hard journey, but it was done under the company motto, "Remember, boys. Nothing on earth must stop the United States mail!" The twenty-eight hundred miles were covered in twenty-four days. This line was abandoned after the Civil War, with the coming of railroads, and was never used again.

Stagecoach drivers were tough, strong, and skillful—like their horses. When bundled up ready for a long winter trip, however, they looked like anything but the picturesque characters you may have seen in the movies! The usual useful but unglamorous costume of a typical driver consisted of a brown corduroy suit, leather leggings and a moth-eaten fur coat tied by a wool scarf around its middle. Two large pistols were stuck into this makeshift belt. Another scarf was tied around the neck and over the ears, while a flat-topped, broad-brimmed felt hat completed the costume.

One of the most famous of the western drivers was a certain Hank Monk. He always kept a cigar in his mouth while he drove, and he was known for his intelligent and considerate handling of his horses. As his coach sped down a treacherous, winding mountain trail, he would sing out to his mustang leaders, "Go long! Go long!" Another famous man, Mark Twain, considered Hank one of the most amusing persons he had ever met. You can read all about him in Mark Twain's book *Roughing It*.

Train and Streetcar Horses

Believe it or not, railroads were used *before* the steam locomotive was invented. The very first railroads were planned in order to help stagecoaches cover the ground faster by having them run on rails instead of over rough roads—or no roads at all. In the early 1800's there were many such railroads in the eastern part of America. They followed the former stagecoach routes, the cars being pulled by horses. They usually consisted of a single car and were hauled by a single horse. When two horses were used they were hitched one behind the other.

The first such railroad cars were simply stagecoaches with their old wheels removed and new ones put on that would cling to tracks. When it was discovered that they could carry twice as many passengers at no extra cost, the lines designed a two-story carriage somewhat like today's double-decker busses. The horses jogged along at quite a good speed, it being fairly easy for them to pull a loaded coach that ran on smooth rails.

Since these early railroads had only one track, there were many accidents. Horses pulling coaches in opposite directions couldn't always stop when they met face to face. Many head-on collisions occurred. But people kept using the newfangled railroad because travel by this method was so much faster and more comfortable than travel by stagecoach. Imagine—these railroad cars often went as fast as *twelve miles an hour!*

Most runs were only about forty or fifty miles long—between cities. When there began to be a demand for traveling greater distances, a problem arose. No horse could pull a coach at a good clip for longer than fifty miles, even a coach on rails. This problem was solved, however, by attaching a flatcar to the passenger car. On this flatcar two spare horses were carried. When the horses that were pulling the train got tired, the spare horses changed places with them. In this way both teams took their turns on the flatcar and had a rest.

Another idea for improved efficiency was to make a car travel over rails—without a horse's *pulling* it. Someone invented a strange vehicle called the "Flying Dutchman." This contraption held ten or twelve passengers and a conductor. It was a flat-topped car with enormous wheels. The passengers sat on benches facing out above the wheels, five or six to a side. Between them was a platform holding a treadmill that was attached to the axles of the wheels. And on this treadmill stood a horse. When it was time for the train to start, the conductor, who stood on a small back platform, cracked his whip. The horse started running at a fast clip. The treadmill went round and round, turning the wheels, while the train moved ahead on the tracks!

The Baltimore and Ohio Railroad tried this invention for a short time, but it never proved to be practical for a very simple reason. The horses were too smart. They got

Years ago horses pulled the streetcars in many cities

tired of running and never going anywhere. They refused to get on the treadmill.

It is possible that the popularity of the horse-drawn railroad hastened the invention and wide use of the steam railroad. But horses were kept handy in case of emergency even after locomotives were put on all railroads. Early steam engines sometimes refused to go when snow or rain dampened their fires, so the engineer would harness a pair of horses to his train in order to finish his run. The only race ever staged between a steam-powered railroad and a horse-drawn railroad was run on a double track in 1830. The horse won!

Long after all railroads were completely powered by steam, however, horses still pulled streetcars in many large cities. Your grandparents may remember having seen one of the last of these horse-drawn trams.

PONY EXPRESS

The Pony Express has been called "the greatest relay race ever run." In a relay race, one runner speeds a lap to the next runner, hands him a stick which that man carries to the next one, and so on until the race is won by the fastest team. That's exactly how the Pony Express raced the mail on horseback across the nineteen hundred miles between St. Joseph, Missouri, and Sacramento, California.

This method of speeding letters across that part of our country which had no railroads was started in 1860. With a shorter route through Denver and Salt Lake City, it was expected the trip could be made faster than by the southwestern route of the Overland Stage Mail. And this proved to be so. The Pony Express made its breath-taking journey in nine or ten days, compared to the twenty-four days it took the stagecoaches. Here's how it was done:

The men selected to be pony riders were excellent horsemen, of course. But they also had to be tough, wiry, serious minded—and weigh only about one hundred and twenty-five pounds. They were paid fifty dollars a month, with food and board, and they were strictly instructed not to fight Indians or each other, not to drink, not to use bad language. Their only job was to get the mail through. This was so difficult that they had little time or strength to rescue damsels in distress, or wipe out a whole Indian tribe singlehanded, as some books or movies have had them do! Like our mailmen today, "neither sleet nor rain nor snow . . ." could keep them from their appointed task.

They rode in any weather and at any hour of the day or night. So that they could ride faster, they always wore the lightest possible clothing—close-fitting shirts, tight pants tucked into boot tops, small hats. There were eighty of these pony riders—forty riding from East to West and forty from West to East. Many of them died performing this important service.

The eighty men used some four or five hundred mustangs. Tough as the men, scrawny, far from beautiful, half wild, these descendants of the Spanish horses ran with the speed of a Thoroughbred—sure footed as a mountain goat. Most of them were as large as cow horses, although they were called ponies. They probably did the hardest work of any horses in the world.

Like their riders, the ponies, too, traveled light. They carried tiny racing saddles with no blankets under them, wearing either the lightest possible iron shoes or none at all. Little flat, leather packets, about the size of a small book, were attached to their saddles. The mail was carried in these packets.

The four or five hundred horses were distributed across the country at some one hundred and ninety relay stations. Two men stayed at these stations to care for the horses there, and to see that one was saddled and ready to go when a rider appeared. A rider galloped at top speed the ten miles between stations.

He blew a horn to warn the men to have a horse waiting for him as he drew near a relay station. Stopping in a cloud of dust, he unhooked the precious mail packets from the saddle of his foam-flecked pony, fastened them to the saddle of the fresh horse, jumped upon his back and was off in another cloud of dust. A rider was allowed only two minutes to make this change—and he had to continue through five stations, or approximately fifty miles, before he could stop for a rest. Then a new man took the mail—and so it was carried all across the plains and mountains to the final stop.

The horse was the real hero of the Pony Express

But it was the horse that was the real hero of the Pony Express. A rider couldn't get the mail through if anything happened to his mount. But the horses could—and often did—carry the mail to the next station without their riders. Sometimes a man would fall off his pony in exhaustion, but the horse went on alone. Swimming rivers, galloping over barren prairies or steep hills, with nothing to guide him but his memory, he carried the mail to the next relay station. This is why the mail packets were attached to the saddle and not to the rider.

Since it cost five dollars to send a letter weighing half an ounce by Pony Express, most such mail was written on tissue paper. Even at this high rate the company found it could not make money. When the Civil War, the telegraph and the railroads came along, therefore, the Pony Express went out of business. It had lasted only a year and a half. But its courageous horses and riders had added an exciting page to the history of this country.

Man's use of the horse to help him till the soil began rather late. Oxen were the animals most used to plow fields in England until the end of the eighteenth century. But after that, the horse started to play an important role in agriculture.

Our colonial settlers brought horses with them and quickly put them to work clearing the forests and plowing the fields. Pennsylvania, which had many Swedish, Finnish and Dutch among its early colonists, soon developed its own large farm horses. Some of these later became the famous Conestoga horses. When European breeds like Percherons, Belgians, Shires and Suffolks were imported, farmers bred and crossbred them to raise

The Belgian is a breed that still works on many farms in the United States

steady, sturdy, reliable work horses. As more and more families moved west into the fertile Mississippi Valley, these horses helped to make our Middle West one of the richest farm areas in the whole world.

In spite of all the mechanized farm tools used today, some seven and a half million horses and mules still work for American farmers. There are good reasons for this continuing popularity of the farm horse, although the time may come when he will no longer be needed.

To date, many farmers have found it cheaper to use horses, because they "live" longer than machinery and can eat the food they help to raise. Tractors, reapers and combines can't run on the corn, hay or alfalfa they help to harvest. They have to have gasoline and oil. And tractors cannot have little tractors! New ones have to be bought when old ones wear out—and this costs a lot of money. Horses can eat what they help grow and have their own colts at little cost to the farmer. Horses can also plow small, hilly fields where the rocky land might ruin a tractor.

Although Percherons, Belgians, Shires and other farm breeds are not as glamorous as their brother cow ponies, race horses or hunters—either in looks or in the work they do—they have made a great and honest contribution to the building of this country. As long as they are used, and probably long afterward, such breeds will be proudly displayed at all middle western state fairs.

The relationship between a farmer and his horse, or between a sharecropper and his mule, is seldom as close as it is between a cowboy and his pony. But one farmer tells about his horse Tony, who particularly disliked the wood ticks that sometimes crawled into his ears. Whenever this happened, Tony came from the pasture to the house. His head shaking from side to side, he looked for the farmer to remove the tick from his skin. He neighed and pawed at the gate until his master came out. Often when plowing, Tony stopped and turned his head until the farmer could reach the ear that had the annoying tick in it. When it was pulled out Tony plodded happily ahead.

Cow Horses

Perhaps more stories have been written, more songs sung and more movies made about our western cow horse than about any other kind of work horse. There is good reason for the popularity of these mustangs, quarter horses, palominos and crossbreds.

In the past, the wild Spanish horses tamed by American Indians enabled them to chase buffalo for their food and fight their enemies for their lives. When explorers began to push into the West they stole or traded for the Indians' horses which they needed. They could not have settled these rich lands without such horses. This was how the Indians' valuable gift of tamed horses was turned against them and used to force them off their own land.

Spaniards were the first foreigners to explore the Southwest. They not only brought horses to America but also contributed its first cattle. Spaniards trained the tamed Indian horses in established methods of cutting, roping, guiding and watching cattle. So Americans have to thank first the Spaniards for giving them the great cattle industry, without which they wouldn't have the meat this big country needs—and then the Indians for giving them the cow ponies, without which they couldn't have the cattle industry.

The same is true in the Argentine, where Gauchos (Argentine cowboys) work the enormous ranches which make that country one of the world's largest beef producers. Probably no mechanical invention can ever take the place of the cow pony, as long as vast herds of cattle are needed to supply basic food.

Cow horses are carefully trained for the work they do. This training begins when they are only six months old. A mustang or quarter horse weanling's first lesson is to learn to wear a rope bridle. This is attached to a long line held by a cowboy on his horse. Slowly and patiently, the cowboy urges his horse ahead, pulling on the line as he tries to get the weanling to follow. Little by little, the baby learns to follow on a rope. When he has been especially obedient he is given a reward of a pinch of salt. This tastes as good to him as candy does to you.

The weanling's next lesson is simply to learn to stand still when his feet are picked up by the cowboy, one by one. This is done so he won't be nervous when the time comes for him to get his first shoes. After he passes this test he is turned loose on the range and allowed to run, play and eat until he is a year old.

The yearling cow pony is taught to walk, trot and canter on a lead line before he gets his first saddle. He is ridden for only a short time at each lesson, but he soon gets used to the new experience and knows he has nothing to fear from the man on his back. Again, he is turned loose to roam the plains with other yearlings until he is about two and a half years old. Now he is big and strong enough to start his final training.

The weanling runs loose on the range until he is a year old

The full-grown cow pony does some of the things he is supposed to do almost instinctively, because he is a "natural-born cow horse" with excellent "cow sense."

He must walk, trot or canter on order. He must learn to come to an instant dead stop from a full gallop. He must be able to turn either to the right or the left in a very small space. He must back up and turn on command. He must be able to make an abrupt turn while moving at high speed, then immediately gallop off in the opposite direction. He must learn to canter in a small figure eight. And he must learn to do all these things, not as tricks, but as essential parts of the daily work he will do.

He must also be able to follow one particular steer in a herd of hundreds. Without his rider's using any ropes, the horse must separate this steer from the others and keep it away from them. This is called "cutting out" and is done when a cowboy has to select one steer from the herd because it is sick or needs to be branded.

In roping, the cow pony must always face the steer or calf that has been cut out, keeping it in position until the cowboy throws his lasso over its head. The horse then pulls back against the rope around the steer's neck. Always facing the steer, no matter where it turns or pulls, always keeping the rope taut between himself and the steer, the horse backs and turns with every move the steer makes. He keeps doing this even after the cowboy dismounts to tie the steer down.

A cow pony is also used as a saddle horse when it comes time for the roundup. Many western ranches are enormous—one, in Texas, is said to be as large as the whole state of Delaware. Cattle are usually allowed to graze all over the range. But twice a year the cowboys ride out to round them up and take them to market. It is a big job for a few cowboys on horses to gather thousands of cattle into one compact group and head them in the direction they want them to go.

First they have to find the cattle on the huge range. Then they have to ride around and around the herd, keeping them together so none is lost as they start to travel toward the fattening pens. The horses have to be as quick as the men to spot a straying steer. They gallop after it and nip at its heels until it is forced to rejoin the herd.

The companionship between a cowboy and his pony is very real. From the day a weanling gets his first lesson to the day he is retired to pasture, a cowboy spends almost all his working hours with his horse. Their job together requires fast thinking and fast action. Both man and horse must think and act in harmony if the job is to be done safely and well.

The oneness of man and horse is the sincere feeling behind many cowboy ballads—like this "Riding Song" which was written by an unknown cowboy to his cow pony:

Let us ride together—
Blowing mane and hair.
Careless of the weather,
Miles ahead of care.
Ring of hoof and snaffle,
Swing of waist and hip,
Trotting down the twisted road
With the world let slip.

Let us laugh together—
Merry as of old,
To the creak of leather
And the morning cold.
Break into a canter;
Shout to bank and tree;
Rocking down the waking trail,
Steady hand and knee.

Take the life of cities—
Here's the life for me.
'Twere a thousand pities
Not to gallop free.
So we'll ride together,
Comrade, you and I,
Careless of the weather,
Letting care go by.

Fire horses had to be strong, fast, faithful and spirited

FIRE HORSES

The wild dash of a fire engine through crowded city streets and past traffic lights—sirens screaming or bells clanging—is exciting to watch. But it was much more exciting in the days when teams of horses pulled the engines, manes and tails flying as they galloped so fast their iron shoes struck sparks from the cobblestones.

The first fire horses pulled their first engines around the middle of the 1800's, and served this purpose for only about sixty years. But they performed a necessary and often heroic service in that short time. London and New York each had about a thousand fire horses, while almost every small town and city had at least one team—which were the community pets. No one particular breed was used, but all fire horses had to be very strong, fast, faithful and spirited. They were usually a Percheron type.

A large firehouse of those days had three wagons: a steam engine to pump water, pulled by three horses . . . a hose reel to carry the long hoses, pulled by two horses . . . and a hook-and-ladder wagon to carry the tall ladders, pulled by one horse. Hanging from the ceiling in front of each wagon was a set of harnesses for the team. This was released with one pull of a cord when the horses stood in place. It fell on their backs and was quickly fastened by a few strong hooks.

Horses lived in open stalls on the first floor of the firehouse, near their wagons and near the wide front door. The men lived on the second floor, sliding down a brass pole to the first floor when the alarm rang. As soon as they heard this, each horse sped from his stall to his own special place before his own wagon, standing still right underneath his own harness. After the men slid down the pole, they ran to release the harness so that it would fall on the horses' backs, fastened it, jumped up onto the seat with reins in hand—and the race to the fire was off before you could say "Jack Robinson."

And it was a race! The horses used every ounce of their strength and speed to reach the fire in record time. They also had to use their brains to stop the heavy steam-engine wagon from running into them when going downhill, or to keep the hook-and-ladder wagon upright as it swerved around corners. All without slowing down a bit. . . . Once at the fire, the horses were unhitched and led to stand in a quiet place until the fire was put out. Then they pulled the wagons back to the station. The horses were the fire *chasers*, while the men were the fire *fighters*. One wasn't much good without the other.

Hundreds of lives and thousands of dollars were saved

because of these powerful, alert animals. When the last of the fire horses made their last run in 1922 in Detroit— the city of the automobile that had taken over their job —many people were truly sorry to see them go.

POLICE HORSES

Mounted policemen are still used in most large cities to control traffic or crowds, and to patrol public bridle paths to stop an occasional runaway.

New York City is especiallly proud of its mounted force, with its carefully chosen and trained horses. While no special breed is required, in order to "join the police" a horse must have the right height, color, disposition and strength. He must be from four to eight years old when he begins his work. He must weigh around one thousand pounds and stand from fifteen to sixteen hands. He must have a long mane and tail, with a coat color of bay. His body must be well built, with good form and strong bones. He must have a nice, free walk and a bold trot— and his disposition must be good. He must be easy to train and have no tendency to bite or kick.

Once a rookie horse meets all these requirements, he is sent to school for three months. This school is deliberately situated in a place with lots of noise around it, in order that the horse may gradually become accustomed to horns, sirens, back-fire explosions, bells, whistles and every kind of city sound. They may make him nervous at first, since he was probably raised in the country. But unless he learns to get used to these strange and frightening noises he can't become a police horse.

Right in the midst of this bedlam he is taught to turn, walk, trot and canter at the spoken command of a trainer who holds him by a long rein and stands on the ground. Then he is saddled and taught to obey the same commands by rein, leg or hand pressure on his body, without any words. He is also taught to jump. Once he has learned to obey these signals, he is then taught to move sideways, crossing his feet one over the other both in front and in back. This is a very difficult thing for a horse to do, and it takes some time for him to learn. But it is a necessary trick in order that the horse will know how to move a crowd of people slowly—yet firmly and safely—in the direction the policeman wants them to go.

When he is letter-perfect in all these lessons, the horse is introduced to the policeman who will ride him as long as they are both in the service. Every effort is made to suit the man to his mount, and the mount to the man, so they will like each other and work well together. The horse must have as much confidence in his rider as the officer has in his horse. He gives his mount a name, puts him through his paces and sees that he is correctly bedded and fed. He also gives him tidbits to reward good behavior, and keeps his feet in good condition. It is the officer's job to make sure his mount's "uniform" of saddle, bridle, bit, girth and stirrups are comfortable and clean. As a result of such good care and companionship, many police horses won't let anyone but their own officers ride them.

The policeman takes his new horse out on real duty at last, showing him how to go near people and walk through them without being afraid or stepping on any toes. He teaches him never to kick or nip at a person or another horse—and to stand where he is left when the officer dismounts. Soon the horse is patrolling a regular beat, guiding traffic or marching in parades like a veteran.

Perhaps the most famous mounted force in the world is the Royal Northwest Mounted Police of Canada. These are the "mounties" who boast that they "always get their man."

Their horses are bred and raised on open ranges in the Canadian Far West. They are a crossbreed of Thoroughbreds and local mares somewhat like American cow ponies. They stand about fifteen hands and weigh around one thousand pounds Until needed for service they roam the ranges—eating grass and sleeping out of doors in all kinds of weather. This makes them exceptionally strong and self-reliant. When the Mounted Police buys them they are brought in from the ranges and broken.

A story is told of a sergeant in this famous unit. When he was out on his regular patrol one winter day, he and his horse got lost in a sudden blizzard. When the storm cleared, the man was horrified to discover that he was snow-blind from the sun's glare on the white countryside. For seven days and nights he lay in one spot—lost, temporarily blinded, starving and almost frozen. His horse stayed with him all that time—living on grass roots which he managed to paw up from beneath the snow. Then one day the horse saw, heard or scented some freight sleighs in the distance. He ran toward them, whinnying urgently to the other horses as if to ask for their help. The drivers of the sleighs couldn't understand his horse-talk, but they did notice that his belly was very swollen because of the pressure of the girth that still held

115

the saddle on his back. Sensing that something must be seriously wrong, the men followed the riderless horse. He led them straight to a mound of snow about a mile and a half away. Partly under this mound lay the sergeant, almost dead of cold and starvation. But his faithful horse had stayed with him to save his life.

CITY HORSES TODAY

The days of glory in honest toil are gone for most city horses. No more spanking Hackney pairs prance proudly down Main Street. No more teams of matched Clydesdales haul enormous brewery wagons with loud ringing of hoofs. No more dashing fire horses.

People who live in cities do see an occasional horse at work, however. Perhaps he pulls an old-fashioned cab driven by a man in old-fashioned livery, for visitors who want to take a leisurely sight-seeing tour. Sometimes he hauls a wagon of fresh flowers, fruits or vegetables from a country market. In a few places, the clip-clop of a milk wagon horse may still be heard in the wee hours of the morning. Most large city parks have stables where three-gaited saddle horses—called park hacks—may be hired by the hour. And of course there are the police horses.

But by and large, the day of the working city horse is past and gone. What labor he still performs in this age of machinery he does mostly in the country and on the ranges. In or near today's cities his main use is to give people pleasure—rather than to labor for them.

PART 5

Horses at Play

CHARIOT HORSES

The early Persians, Assyrians and Greeks all had the idea of using horses for enjoyment as well as for work. But it was the Romans who seem to have used them primarily for sports. And it is the Roman chariot race, as described in such books as *Ben Hur*, that shows most clearly how horses of ancient days gave people pleasure.

The powerful, fast chariot horses and their drivers were organized into teams like baseball clubs today, and the Circus Maximus in Rome was their Yankee Stadium. This enormous arena held nearly two hundred and fifty thousand spectators, with a special box for the Emperor. Men selling food, drinks and cushions climbed up and down the circular stone benches crying their wares. People cheered when the umpire stood in the center of the field to announce the entries in a race.

This race was a wild affair. The driver stood in a small, two-wheeled chariot whose sides came up only to his knees. He held a whip in one hand. The reins attached to

117

his four- or six-horse team were tied around his waist and held in the other hand. A sharp knife was carried in the belt around his short, white toga.

The chariots all lined up along one side of the oval course around which they had to run seven times to the finish. The umpire dropped a flag—and the race started with a crack of whips, a screech of wheels and the pounding of many hoofs. All went smoothly as long as the horses galloped down the straightaway. But when they reached the turns of the oval the chariots jammed together as each driver tried desperately to be the first one around. Smash-ups were so unavoidable at every curve that there were always accidents. Whenever a chariot overturned in the crush, and the rider was thrown to the ground, he quickly cut the reins with his knife before his horses could drag him around the rest of the course. For the horses kept going—with or without their driver, with or without a chariot, even without each other when teams broke apart.

It was this bloodthirsty, thrilling clash of chariots and struggling horses that the crowd enjoyed more than the race itself. The finish was often so wild and confused that the spectators never did see which team won. But they took the umpire's word for this, going home with throats sore from much yelling. The horses returned to their stables exhausted—and frequently injured. They were fed a good dinner and their wounds were cared for, so they would be strong and well enough to run another hard, dangerous race the next day.

Polo is very much like a game of hockey that is played on horseback. It is an ancient game that is believed to have been played first in Persia.

In the sixth century B.C., the story goes, the King of Persia grew angry at Alexander the Great's continual warfare. So he sent the young Greek general a present of a polo ball and mallet, with the message that a boy of his age might be happier playing games than playing at war. Alexander thanked the King with the reply that the ball was the earth and he, Alexander, was the mallet—which was his way of warning the King that he intended to conquer the whole world.

Although no one knows exactly when or where the game of polo originated, its popularity spread from Persia to Turkey, Tibet, China and India. There are pictures painted at the time of the Mogul invasion of India that show polo being played even at night. With torches placed around the field, the players used a ball of pitch or tar that had been set afire. They galloped over the dark field toward the torchlighted goal posts, knocking this dangerous object with their mallets as they swung down from their horses' backs.

From India, British sportsmen brought the game to England and Ireland about a hundred years ago. Today in America it is played almost exactly the same as it was played in Persia long ago.

The modern game of polo is played on a field that is three hundred yards long and one hundred and fifty yards wide. This is fenced along its sides by a low barrier in order to keep the ball within the playing area. At each end of the field are goal posts, like football goals, only made of light wood so the horses won't be injured if they crash into them.

There are four players on each team. Each player has to have a string of extra ponies ready for replacements, however, because no one horse has the endurance to play through an entire game. Mounts are changed between periods. Each player holds a long mallet made of light, pliable wood, with a tapered head and a leather thong at the handle to go around his wrist. The balls, made of English willow, painted white, are ten inches around and weigh four ounces. It takes great skill to hit one with the small mallet-head from the back of a galloping horse—especially when three or four other players are trying to do the same thing at the same time!

The men wear boots, white riding breeches and shirts and a white helmet cap that protects their heads from injury. The ponies wear lightweight saddles and equipment, so they can move very fast. They usually have their manes hogged, so long hair can't catch in the flying mallets. Their tails are either docked or bandaged, for the same reason. Their legs are wrapped in white puttees from knee to pastern. This is to prevent their being hurt by a hard-driven ball or a swinging mallet. After a pony has finished playing he is taken to his stable, given a liniment rubdown and inspected for possible wounds.

The players of the two teams are matched against each other by positions, as in hockey. The Number One and Number Two players act as forwards and do most of the offensive work. The Number Three players are sort of half-backs who are both defensive and offensive. And the Number Fours are the backs who guard the goals and send the balls away from them toward the opposite goal posts.

The game begins when an official tosses the ball into the middle of the field between the two opposing forwards. Each period of play, called a chukker, lasts seven and a half minutes. There are six chukkers to a game. The team that drives the most balls between their enemy's goal posts in that time wins the game.

Polo is a tough, skillful, exciting game. The horses seem to enjoy it as much as the men, but it takes time and patience to develop a good polo pony. A beginner pony first has to get used to the mallets and balls, since he must not show the slightest sign of fear of them during a game. These are hung in his stall for many weeks, and the pony's only lesson is to become used to them. Next, the mallet is swung gently to and fro before his eyes to teach him that this strange object will not harm him.

When he is taken out for his first riding lesson in the game, the mallet is then whirled around his head and under his body until he is so unafraid of it that he no longer pays it any attention, no matter what his rider does.

A rubber ball is sometimes used for these training sessions, so the pony won't be hurt if it hits him. It is very important for him to learn never to shy away from the ball. For the same reason, the rider must always loosen the reins at the exact moment he hits a ball, in order to prevent his mount from associating a painful jerk on his mouth with this act. Soon the pony keeps his eye on the ball as he chases it—with the mallet whistling about his ears.

Next, the pony must learn to do this with other ponies

about him. He must not be nervous when horses come near him. Eventually, he must be trained to rush right into them when it is necessary to pursue the ball or block a play. He is introduced to a game between two teams after he has learned these things.

This practice game, however, is played much more slowly than a real one. The pony is held down to a canter until he learns all the tricks of the trade. Only when he is an expert at this gait is he allowed to participate in a galloping practice game. It is easy to see from all these requirements why a good polo pony is so valuable to his owner.

Polo ponies can't play their strenuous game for very long. They are honorably retired to a comfortable pasture while still young. They are given excellent care even then, because fine polo ponies can usually become the fathers or mothers of equally fine polo pony colts.

An odd thing happened in a game of polo that was being played in Mexico City between an American and a Mexican team. An American player hit the ball such a hard blow that it split into two parts. One part was blocked by the Mexican back, but the other part went between the goal posts. The umpire couldn't decide whether the Americans had scored a goal or not. He was very puzzled until he got the idea of measuring the two parts of the broken ball. Because he found that the larger part was the one that had gone between the goal posts, he finally decided that the Americans had scored. They won the game seven to six because of this decision.

There are three popular ways to race a horse for spectators. Each way uses a different kind of race track and different types of horses. The first way is a run over a bare straight or circular course, and is the kind of racing done by Thoroughbreds ridden by jockeys. The second way is to drive horses attached to little carts over a flat course. This is the kind of racing done by trotting or pacing Standardbreds. And the third way is to race mounts over a course that is covered with various obstacles. This is the steeplechase.

The steeplechase originated in England many years ago as a cross-country race from a certain starting point to a church steeple a number of miles away. This is how such a race got its name. The horses, usually hunters, had to run across the land—leaping over any natural barriers they found in their way. Ability to jump without falling was more important than speed, and such races became very popular with the fox-hunting English who enjoyed this type of riding.

In Queen Victoria's time, a circular steeplechase course was built outside the village of Aintree, near Liverpool. It was laid out to imitate cross-country conditions, with grandstands from which spectators could watch. The annual event still held here is known as the Grand National. It is perhaps the most famous steeplechase in the world. America, too, has its well-known steeplechases, two of which are the New York Handicap and the Maryland Cup.

Steeplechasing is a dangerous sport. Horses specially trained for this kind of racing are usually large Thor-

Horses trained for steeplechasing are usually Thoroughbreds with lots of stamina

oughbreds who have shown exceptional stamina and jumping ability. They need these qualities to finish a steeplechase course! The average race is more than two miles long and contains many fences of different heights, some of wood, some of hedge. There are deep, six-foot-wide ditches with four-foot fences in front of them, and water ditches twelve feet wide, with three-foot fences before them.

Good as the horses must be, their jockeys are very important, too. Unless a rider senses when to help the horse take off for a jump—and when to lean back to balance as the horse lands—there is always a chance of a spill. Some people claim that bad jockeys cause more falls than bad horses. Every now and then a steeplechaser finishes a race without a single stumble—after his jockey has fallen off! There are always many spills during a steeplechase, and often the horse or jockey or *both* are seriously hurt.

The training of steeplechasers is also important. Although a few horses are natural jumpers, most of them have to be taught. This is a long process that calls for a lot of patience. Unlike Thoroughbred racing horses, a steeplechaser doesn't even begin his training until he is four years old. This is because he is not strong enough to start real jumping until then. The best steeplechasers are usually between ten and thirteen years old when they win races.

Fox Hunting

Fox hunting is also called "riding to hounds," and it is almost the only way the horse is still used for hunting. Such hunting is a sport, not a necessity, but it is not as cruel as it may seem. For the fox is a sneaky creature that lives by raiding chicken houses or eating baby rabbits in their burrows. In a fox hunt he is given a fair chance to escape his pursuers.

Many hundreds of acres of special land are needed to hold a fox hunt with a real fox, since the wily animal covers lots of ground—and the huntsmen can hardly gallop roughshod over a farmer's wheat field as they follow him. If they do not own enough of this special, uncultivated land, hunt clubs often hold what they call a "drag hunt." In this hunt, a man on horseback drags the scent of a fox over the hunt property ahead of the hunters, but there is no animal to be killed at the end of the chase. A drag hunt is just as much fun for the horses and riders as the real thing, however, since it is their job to follow wherever the hounds' noses lead them. And a merry chase that can be—up hill, down dale, across brooks and over fences . . . until the hounds reach home again to find they have been trailing only a fox-scented piece of burlap instead of a real fox!

As there is no way for spectators to watch this sort of cross-country race that covers many miles and takes many hours, fox-hunting is a sport only for those who ride in it. And since it costs a lot of money to own and train the horses and hounds—and to buy the special riding habits and the land where the hunt can be safely held—it is mainly a sport for rich people. It is most popular in England, Ireland and America.

There are many old-fashioned prints of huntsmen riding to hounds in their pink coats. These coats are really red, but it is said that they began to be called pink in the days when a tailor named Mr. Pyncke used to make most of the hunting coats for the English nobility.

They make a fine picture—the glossy horses and their brightly dressed riders grouped together in the faint dawn light as they wait for the cry "View hallo!" which means the fox has been sighted. The yapping, excited hounds get the scent, then off they go, the huntsmen galloping after them, scarlet backs flying over fences, hedges and green fields.

A good hunter is really a good jumping race horse. He has no interest at all in the fox or the fox scent. His business is simply to follow the baying hounds as fast as he can, leaping over any obstacle in his path. The most important quality he must have is the ability to stretch his legs and body when taking a jump. This is called "scope."

The glossy hunters and their brightly dressed riders make a fine sight

It enables the horse safely to get over a barrier that may be wider than it looked to be from the other side. He must also have plenty of spunk to continue the hunt to its very end.

This old English story shows what kind of pluck a hunter has to have:

Toward the end of a long, trying chase, the fox's trail led across a small river. A horse named Spring jumped the river all right, but as he landed on the opposite bank he fell. When his rider managed to rise to his feet he saw Spring floating down the river, all four hoofs in the air. He thought the poor horse was a goner for sure. Just then, however, he saw him turn over. Calling another huntsman to help, they dragged the horse to land.

Spring was so weak he staggered like a newborn foal. But as his rider was leading him back toward his stable and a veterinarian, the distant baying of the hounds was heard. Spring pricked up his wet ears. The hounds came closer. Spring fidgeted with his wet feet. His rider mounted him to keep him calm. Then the pack of hounds appeared right in front of them.

Spring was off in a gallop. All his pains were forgotten as he sped across fields and meadows, leaping fences like a colt. After a run of some eight or ten miles, he brought his master right to the kill at the end of the hunt. When the excitement was over it was discovered that Spring had lost two shoes, had one eye closed and was bleeding from a bad wound in his jaw which he had received when he fell. Of course he needed good care and a long rest before he hunted again. But nothing could have stopped him from following those hounds!

Oddly enough, this is the sport and this is the kind of riding that real fox hunters like best, both man and horse.

RACING

Flat Racing

The kind of horse racing popular today was not a particularly popular sport in ancient times. The earliest-known English races took place at the horse market of Smithfield. They were not so much races as demonstrations of horses' running ability for prospective buyers. Later, races between knights' coursers were held for the public. The king, Henry VIII, was an enthusiastic horseman. He encouraged the breeding of fine horses and the running of races. Such early races were often four to six miles long, while today's are seldom more than a mile and a half. James I began the real breeding of light horses especially for racing. Ever since his day England has been one of the top countries for raising the Thoroughbred race horses that originated there.

The Derby is one of the best-known races in the world. It is held on Epsom Downs in Surrey, England. Long ago the mineral waters around this spot had attracted many visitors (this is where Epsom Salts came from), and several large hotels were built to accommodate them. Around 1780 Lord Derby sponsored a race held there, giving it his name and attracting still more people to the little village. Every year since then, spectators have come from all over the world to see the running of this famous race.

The wearing of bright-colored jackets and caps—to show who owned the horses that were racing—began around 1750. Lord Derby registered his jockey's colors —black with white cap—in 1799. Since all other solid colors were quickly assigned to different stables, striped, squared, polka-dotted and other varicolored shirts and caps had to be used as more and more people began to race their horses. The sky-blue-and-brown cap of the Whitney stables are probably America's oldest racing colors.

From being the "sport of kings," horse racing became a big business. In the United States there are over fifty thousand Thoroughbreds registered in the Jockey Club, the association which keeps the records of this breed. Of these, some thirteen thousand run races every year to

Horse racing, once called the "sport of kings," has become popular in America

compete for prizes that total about ten million dollars. Huge grandstands and well-kept tracks exist in almost every state of the union, while thousands of people attend the races. The most famous of these, like the Kentucky Derby, the Preakness or the Belmont Stakes, are broadcast on radio and television. While only the best horses in the country are entered in these events, many millions of dollars are spent each year in breeding and training the Thoroughbreds that might possibly be good enough to win one of the big prizes. Farms for race horses have their own practice tracks, acres of land for exercise paddocks and raising food, many stud horses, brood mares, colts and yearlings, as well as a staff of professional trainers and jockeys.

Calumet Farms, near Lexington, Kentucky, is one of the best known of all racing stables. Horses bred and trained here have won close to a million dollars in a single year for their owner. It has produced such famous champions as Whirlaway and Citation.

There is an amusing true story about Citation. He was the "horse of the year" in 1948, since he had won almost all the biggest races of that season. When it came time to hold a race called the Pimlico Special, all other owners refused to enter their horses in this event because they were sure that Citation would beat them. So when the race was to be run, Citation was the only horse to walk calmly out to the starting post, jockey on his back. The starter dropped a flag and off Citation went—galloping around the whole course to the finish line. The crowd cheered him as loudly as if he had just beaten ten other fast horses, instead of running all by himself!

The raising and training of such famous horses is a serious affair that begins even before a foal is born. His father and mother are carefully selected for him. When a colt is about six months old he is taken away from his mother and weaned. Then his real training begins. He has to get used to having people and other horses about him. He has to learn to walk in a circle at the end of a lead line, doing what his trainer tells him to do. As he walks, another man keeps one hand on his back, so the colt will gradually get used to the feeling of a weight there. Then a saddle is put on him and a jockey mounts him for the first time in order to teach him to carry a rider.

When he is a year old he is taught to answer the reins and to run slowly. Yearlings go to school in the morning and are turned out to run in pastures at night, when the weather is warm. Keeping colts or fillies together in one paddock helps them grow strong as they play with each other. It also gives them confidence in being near other horses.

A good yearling will often be wild spirited. The most effective way to calm him down seems to be by use of the human voice. Many excellent trainers will put a so-called "wild" horse in his stall, then just stand near by and talk to him softly for hours. That is why, when you meet a strange horse for the first time, you should always talk to him before you pet him. This will help win his confidence, without which you will never win his affection. Horses don't seem to become attached to people as easily as dogs do.

A yearling gets his first shoes on his eighteen-month birthday, after which he is made acquainted with the farm's race track. Here he gallops with other yearlings, running first one way around the course, then turned by his trainer to run the other way. Next he is taught to get used to the starting gates, so he won't be frightened by this strange barrier and will get off to a fast start in a real race without balking, bucking, rearing or shying. Then he is introduced to the trailer in which he will travel all over the country to different race tracks. He quickly learns to ride in his "car" without becoming scared, after he has been led up and down its ramp several times.

A young race horse is always rubbed down or walked near a place where automobiles and people constantly pass. In this way he gets accustomed to the sounds of an actual track, so that they will not make him nervous right before a big race. He does not enter a real race until he is two years old.

Most owners of race horses also have what they call "lead ponies" in their stables. These wise little horses serve a valuable purpose. They are used to teach a yearling the tricks of racing. During practice races on the farm track, they gallop alongside the youngster to show him where to pull up. They will even pin him against the rail if he gets too fresh. These same ponies lead the racer onto the track at an actual race. This gives the high-strung Thoroughbred confidence and keeps him calm up to the starting gate. After a race has been run, the job of a lead pony and his rider is to go after the excited racer, quiet him down and lead him back to his stall.

A good Thoroughbred can race and earn money to repay his owner for his upbringing for many years. Budweiser II won races when he was seventeen years old, and others have raced at ten, twelve, or fourteen years. After their racing days are over, a good stallion or mare retires on the farm to raise families of other Thoroughbreds. Man o' War, one of the greatest champions of them all, fathered many famous colts until he died at the grand old age of thirty.

In addition to the cost of his education, the physical care of a race horse is expensive. The average Thoroughbred eats about twenty pounds of hay, nine quarts of oats and two quarts of bran a day, when he is working. His feet, legs, general health and looks must be cared for daily. Sometimes this care takes extreme forms. One trainer took his string of racers to a Florida beach after a hard season. There he turned them loose and let them swim in the salt water for an hour or two each day. He claimed that the swimming straightened out the horses' tired muscles, while the change of scene improved their tempers and dispositions. And in Buenos Aires, where racing is also a most popular sport, the Argentine Jockey Club has a specially built rectangular swimming pool. Besides it stands a sign that reads, FOR HORSES ONLY!

Racing fans really love their favorites, often giving them nicknames. Man o' War was always called Big Red because he was large and had a reddish coat. Stymie, a famous horse that won most of the large prizes of his day, was nicknamed Moneybags. And Exterminator, one of the world's best, was so ugly that he was affectionately but laughingly called "Old Bones."

Of all the hundreds of queer names given to race horses, two are perhaps outstandingly odd. One was the name given to a horse in England over a hundred years ago. His name was Potatoes. As if this weren't funny enough, a mistake made it even funnier. It seems the owner told a stableboy to print the name and put it over the horse's stall. Because the boy didn't know how to spell very well, he printed POT-o-o-o-o-o-o-o's. And ever since then, this horse's name has been registered as "POT-8-o's."

The other strange name was recently given to a Thoroughbred colt whose owners apparently are TV fans. They named him Uncle Miltie!

Harness Racing

Harness racing is not really a very old sport, although it might be said to have started with the Roman chariot races. As was explained in the description of Standardbred horses, this kind of racing is done by trotters and

134

pacers who pull drivers in small, light carriages called sulkies.

This is a truly American sport which is as down to earth and cheap as Thoroughbred racing is fancy and expensive. It began when farmers in the early eighteenth century used to race each other's horses and carriages along country roads. This was called "brushing." It became so popular that it was soon organized into a regular sport on a regular track, with its own rules and regulations.

In 1806 a horse named Yankee won one of the first of these trotting races at Harlem, New York. With the perfection of the Standardbred breed, such races became increasingly popular. In the United States today some fifteen million people a year watch harness races on six hundred tracks throughout the country. The most famous trotting race in the world is the Hambletonian, run at Goshen, New York.

A trotting or pacing race is usually a mile long. It is run over a smooth dirt course that is circular in shape. The sulkies are sometimes started in assigned places behind a special automobile that has two long arms which form a gate on each side of it. When they reach the starting line, the car speeds ahead of the horses, down the middle of the track, while the gate arms fold back out of the way. The car leaves the course and the sulkies dash by, wire wheels flashing as they turn to the regular beat of the horses' hoofs.

Each driver carries a stop watch to time his horse's speed, holding him back until the last stretch to the finish. Every horse must stay on gait—trot, if he is a trotter (see page 67), or pace, if he is a pacer (see page 67) —since trotters race against other trotters and pacers against pacers. If he switches gaits (goes from trot to pace or from pace to trot) he is disqualified, no matter how fast he has run. If he loses stride or breaks into a gallop for a moment, the driver must get his sulky out of the way, then urge his horse back into his regular gait. He is disqualified for this only if the officials judge that he got ahead of the others while his horse galloped.

Training a Standardbred to keep his gait at top speed requires much time and patience. While a Thoroughbred is considered in his prime at three years old, a harness horse does not start his training until he is two years old —and he is at his best at around six. Goldsmith Maid, one of the greatest trotters, was never even broken to harness until she was six—and didn't begin to race until she was eight.

This famous mare was very temperamental. She refused to run a race unless her pet stablemate, a little yellow dog, was somewhere on the course. She devoured enormous quantities of hay before each race. She seemed to know just when a race was to be run, for her hoofs would chatter on the stable floor like a person's teeth chatter in fear or excitement. But no one could make her race if she didn't feel like it, or stop her from racing if she wanted to. She became very calm as soon as she was led out onto the track. From that moment on, she ran her own race, judging when to spurt ahead and when to hold back. No driver could interfere with her decisions. She won 116 out of 138 races, earning $336,000 in prize money. She broke a world's record when she was seventeen and raced until she was twenty. To achieve such startling results takes expert training, however.

Good trainers know their horses like a mother knows

her children. After a Standardbred learns how to lead to halter, he is trained to wear harness and pull a cart. It usually takes about a month for him to get used to his trainer and to pulling a sulky. Next he is taught to trot or to pace, depending upon which gait he naturally does best. He is kept down to a slow speed during this training.

He often wears head poles to keep him from turning his head, or knee boots, ankle wraps and hobbles to improve his particular gait. This is when he is fitted to his shoes. They are changed many times until the trainer finds just the right combination of weight and balance to help the horse keep an even stride with the least amount of effort.

The last phase of his training is to teach him to trot or pace faster—by workouts every day—until he has achieved that perfection of speed and sure, easy gait which shows he is ready for a race. To buy, train, feed and equip a good harness horse, however, costs only about one tenth of what it costs to bring up a Thoroughbred.

Harness-racing drivers are colorful in a different way from the tiny jockeys who ride Thoroughbreds. They are mostly older men, some farmers, some horse-breeders, none very wealthy. Balanced on the small sulky seats, reins in hands, goggles over their eyes, they take their racing as seriously as any jockey—and they need every bit as much courage and intelligence as he does, too. They also wear their stables' bright-colored silk jackets, with matching caps on their gray heads.

One of the most famous of all harness racers is a woman. She is sixty-seven years old and has seven children and three grandchildren. Her name is Mrs. Forrest

Burrights, but the racing fans all call her Grandma. She and her husband sleep in the barns when their horses are racing at a state fair or at an important harness race. She drives twenty-five or thirty races a season, usually winning more than half of them. Some of her sons and daughters have also become famous drivers.

Another noted driver is a young lady named Alma Shepard. When she was only eleven years old she drove a trotter for the fastest mile ever run by a female driver!

CIRCUS HORSES

Perhaps as long as there are circuses there will be circus horses. Indeed, the earliest circuses in history were nothing but acts of trick riding or trick horses. Back in the days of the Roman Empire, riders did feats on horseback —running races in which they jumped from one horse to another, or standing up on the backs of two horses, holding long reins in their hands. During the Middle Ages in Europe there were traveling troupes that entertained the public with acrobatic acts on horseback while their horses trotted around a circle in a field. In Queen Elizabeth's time the special amusement at street corners or crossroads was to watch trained horses doing their stunts.

In the eighteenth century, regular circuses that visited different towns and villages were formed. Their acts were done entirely with horses who performed in a circle of ropes tied to stakes. One poster of this time announced

SEE A LITTLE LADY ONLY EIGHT YEARS OLD
WHO RIDES TWO HORSES AT FULL GALLOP,
ENOUGH TO PUT ANYONE IN FITS WHO SEES HER!

Another poster boasted of

A SON OF A PERSON OF QUALITY
WHO RIDES AT FULL SPEED
WITH HIS RIGHT FOOT IN THE SADDLE
AND HIS LEFT TOE IN HIS MOUTH!

Still another handbill in London in the 1880's advertised

PROFESSOR CROCKER'S PERFECTLY EDUCATED HORSES,
WHO CAN DO EVERYTHING BUT TALK!

The advertisement continued:

HORSES AT SCHOOL
HORSES AS BELL RINGERS
HORSES PLAYING SEESAW
HORSES DISTINGUISHING COLORS
HORSES AS SOLDIERS
HORSES AT COURT
HORSES AT BATTLE

In eighteenth-century America, too, horses were the only features of a circus. It wasn't until later that clowns, acrobats and other performers were added. Even today, when the horse acts hold a much less important place, most circus performers rate the bareback riders at the very top of their profession. They know that no matter how sensational other acts may look, it is the bareback tricks that require the most skill.

Just as the riders must be highly trained, so the horses used for this difficult art must be very special. Although what they actually do seems monotonous and simple, it is really the result of careful training. Horses chosen for this work can be of any breed—as long as they have broad backs for the riders to stand on.

As long as there are circuses, there will be circus horses

Percheron types, ponies or western horses are used—
and they are nearly always white. They must also be intelligent and beautiful, with a rather heavy body and a
calm disposition. They are taught to canter round and
round the ring without breaking the steady rhythm or
speed. They must also keep their minds on their work
—never becoming distracted or frightened by the antics
of clowns or the noises made by the audience.

A bareback horse's two greatest assets are a steady
canter and steady nerves. Without them, the riders could

not do a single one of their astonishing stunts. A bareback rider must always be able to count on his horse. He must know precisely where he will be at a certain split second. If he didn't, he could never do the somersaults that are so thrilling to watch—the backward, the forward-forward, and the backward-back. In this last trick, the rider stands on the horse's back, facing the rear. He throws himself into the air in a backward somersault, then lands on the horse's back. This is very difficult because while the rider is in the air the horse is moving forward and away from him. The rider must throw himself back with great strength in order to land on the spot to which the horse has cantered during the somersault. A rider who can do this trick can get almost any salary he demands.

A circus horse also learns how to walk on his hind feet, dance as the band keeps time to his steps, then bow to the spectators. Strange as it seems, however, these tricks are easier to teach him than the unglamorous, steady cantering around the ring. He is also often a part of the "Living Statues," where people and animals—painted white and wearing white clothes—hold a picture position while the platform on which they stand slowly turns under a soft blue light. Needless to say, it takes great patience to teach the horse not to move a muscle until the curtain falls.

A circus horse plays an important part in parades that wind through towns to announce the arrival of the circus. Not so long ago, these colorful parades were almost as exciting as the show itself. In addition to the beautiful white performing horses that marched, powerful work horses pulled the band wagons. At one time these horses were the biggest attraction of the entire parade. Mr. Bailey, of the famous Barnum and Bailey partnership, had the idea of hitching forty horses into one team to pull an enormous wagon. The team was made up of ten lines of huge Percherons marching four abreast. Altogether, they weighed about eighty thousand pounds! With twenty reins attached to them, one single driver controlled and guided this greatest team of horses ever seen. And what a fine sight it must have been—forty horses, their heads decorated with red plumes, trotting slowly down a narrow, cobblestone street, the proud driver perched high above them on the red-and-gold band wagon!

RODEO

A rodeo is a purely American kind of circus that brings the wild West to people who couldn't otherwise see it. In its original form it was simply an expert exhibition of the kind of work cowboys and their ponies do on ranches, but many trick performances have been added to it, making this a most exciting show to watch—or in which to take part.

About seven hundred rodeos are staged in the United States every year, with some two thousand professional cowboys appearing in them. These men receive no salary except prize money if they win an event. They are often seriously hurt and usually have to retire from this strenuous sport before they're thirty years old. But they seem to enjoy their risky work while they can still do it!

Some of the things they must do are difficult or dangerous or both—and their cow ponies have to be almost as smart as the riders. One contest is calf-roping. A calf must be lassoed from horseback, then tied by the cowboy on the ground while his pony holds the rope taut. The cowboy who does this in the fastest time wins the prize. There are prizes, too, for the best cutting horse and the best steer-roping. Yet the horses who attract the most attention in a rodeo are not the intelligent, hard-working ponies who do these jobs, but the useless flashy broncos.

Broncs are mustangs who have never been broken to saddle. They simply will not tolerate a man on their back. Yet it is the cowboy's aim to ride for at least ten seconds on one of these bucking, jumping, side-stepping, explosive animals. While he's sticking on the bronc's back with all his might, he also has to obey these rules: Scratch the horse from stem to stern with spurs . . . hold the halter six inches above the horse's neck with one hand while fanning the sky with the other . . . keep both feet in the stirrups . . . and don't grab hold of anything but the reins.

Or a cowboy may enter the contest to see who can ride an equally wild Brahman bull for eight seconds while following the same rules. He must be very careful not to get gored by a horn when he either falls or jumps off the enraged animal.

Another popular rodeo event is a race in which wild horses compete. Eight unbroken horses are released from stalls at one end of the arena. A team of three men handles each horse, two men holding the bucking beast on a long rein while the third man saddles and mounts (!) it. He then rides to the finish line at the far end of the arena. The team that manages to get its horse there first wins the race.

Rodeo riders are as famous to rodeo fans as movie stars are to movie fans. Dick Griffith is a thirty-three-year-old Arizona cowboy who became world champion trick rider at the age of nine. He had started doing tricks on his Shetland pony when he was only six years old. His most famous trick today is to leap on the backs of two running horses, one foot on each horse. Holding only a single rein on each jumper, with no connecting rein between the two horses, he then guides the pair to jump over an automobile.

Women are excellent rodeo performers, too. One of the best known is Tad Lucas, who is the mother of still another feminine rider, aged nineteen. Tad Lucas originated the stunt called the "back drag." She slips her feet through straps on the back of her saddle. With her horse galloping at full speed, she then hangs head down over his tail. Her head almost touches the ground right by the horse's heels before she throws herself back up into the saddle.

The horses in a rodeo also earn fame. One of the greatest of these was a jet-black "bad" horse named Midnight. Cowboys claim that a "bad" horse can't be made; he must be born that way. No one can teach a bronc the sudden corkscrew turns or bucks that keep a rider from sticking in the saddle—and a truly tricky bronc is respected by the cowboys as well as by the audience.

Midnight was such a bronc. But he didn't start out to be one. For quite a while Midnight quietly and sedately pulled the buggy owned by a schoolteacher in Canada. One day a wheel came off the buggy. In order not to be late, the teacher decided to ride Midnight to school. He unhitched his placid horse, climbed on his back—and

144

that was the last thing he remembered until he came to ten minutes later, lying in a cloud of dust.

After that experience the teacher never dared drive or ride Midnight again, so he entered him in a rodeo. This began Midnight's career as the greatest bucker in the world. When he died, cowboys put up a monument over his grave which read:

BENEATH THIS SOD LIES A GREAT BUCKING HOSS—
THERE NEVER LIVED A COWBOY HE COULDN'T TOSS.
HIS NAME WAS MIDNIGHT, HIS COAT BLACK AS COAL—
IF THERE'S A HOSS HEAVEN, PLEASE, GOD, REST HIS SOUL

Rodeos are now becoming a regular feature of college sports in some places. There are thirty-five rodeo teams in eleven of our western states. Most of the students at these colleges come from cow country and have been riding since they could walk. They are experts at all the regular rodeo stunts. They take their own horses to school, wear shirts with the college colors—and travel to compete against other school teams, just as college football, swimming or basketball teams do. When they graduate, most of the riders expect to go into some form of the ranching business, and they study to prepare for this while at college. Some people think college rodeos will soon be as popular in the West as the big college football games now are.

HORSE SHOWS AND STATE FAIRS

Horses are judged at shows and fairs on the basis of two main things: their looks, health and general physical

145

conformation to their particular breed—and the performance of their particular work. Although horse shows were originally restricted to rather wealthy audiences who could afford to own, breed and train blooded horses, this is no longer true. Thousands of people attend horse shows who have never ridden or who never hope to own even a burro. They go out of love for horses and the pleasure of seeing them perform.

The National Horse Show, the most famous in the world, fills New York's Madison Square Garden during a week of events. The first National was held in the 1880's for the purpose of improving the breeding of horses. It has been held every year since, attracting the best of horses and horsemen and the most enthusiastic of audiences. As many as four hundred horses are entered in one or another of the classes under the five divisions of the show. These divisions are: harness horses, hunters, saddle horses, jumpers and military.

In the harness class Hackneys, Standardbreds or other light harness breeds are exhibited singly or in teams, pulling different styles of carriages. The equipment of the carriage, the costume of the driver—even the harness itself—are all judged as strictly as the horses. Everything must be just so. The turnouts make a beautiful picture as they roll over the tanbark with all woodwork gleaming and every bit of silver, chrome or brass shining. Of course the horses are gleaming and shining, too, for they are judged, not for their speed, but for their appearance, the way they keep the same regular, prancing gait, their obedience in answering their driver's reins.

In judging hunters, a course is laid out in the arena which resembles, as much as possible, the actual con-

Saddle horses are interesting to watch at a horse show

ditions of a real fox hunt. Entries are fine horses that are
experienced hunters, while their riders must be dressed
exactly as if riding to hounds—pink coats and all. The
horses are judged on their looks and their ability to jump
the various obstacles. The riders are judged on their riding habits and their ability to handle their mounts.

Saddle horse classes are among the most interesting
events to watch. Here are exhibitions of riding and
saddle horses at their best—men and women in smart
habits, their mounts curried, brushed and combed until

147

they fairly glitter. Horse and rider are judged as a unit on performance and looks. In a three-gaited class they show at a walk, a trot and a canter. In a five-gaited class they show at a walk, a running walk, a trot, a rack and a canter. To the average eye, every entry behaves so correctly and looks so glamorous that it seems impossible for the judges ever to decide which horse should win first prize.

In the jumping division, more attention is paid to performance than to appearance, since good looks will not help a horse get over a high fence. Different barriers of different heights are placed around the ring. One by one, the jumpers exhibit how well they can leap them. Points are scored against a horse that touches, knocks down or disobeys. Touching the top rail of a jump with the front hoofs is more serious than touching it with the hind hoofs. Knocking down a part of the barrier, falling—or causing his rider to fall—counts more heavily. And disobedience—a jumper's persistent refusal to take a jump —is the worst score against him. He is given three chances to take a jump. If he still refuses he is removed from the competition.

The military division is probably the most colorful event. It is held on the last night of the National. Any country can enter a team of four horses and riders in this class. France, England, Belgium, Canada, Chile, Mexico and Ireland have all sent teams at one time or another. The arena is arranged to look like a battlefield, with obstacles like a tent, a cannon, stacked rifles and a wall with sandbags on its top. Each team of four must run over this course once, jumping every barrier within one minute and ten seconds. The team that does this the fastest— with the fewest knockdowns, touches or disobediences—

wins the trophy. In this event the horses are judged only on their ability to clear the jumps clearly and quickly.

Horses are also exhibited at state fairs during the summer and fall months. During the days, exhibits of Percherons, Shires, Clydesdales and other large work horses are held. They are judged on their health, looks and on how they meet the standards of their breeds, without having to perform any work. In the evenings, however, a "society" horse show takes place, usually with harness and saddle horse classes which are judged in the same manner as in larger shows.

Exhibits of stock horses display mustangs, quarter horses, palominos and other stock breeds at work. In some contests each horse must gallop to a dead stop within a short distance . . . turn figure eights at a canter . . . back up and turn on command . . . then hold still when his rider throws a rope—as if lassoing a steer—and dismounts. In other contests they must gallop between barrels spaced down a track—without touching them. The stock horses that do these things the best win the prizes. The competition is exciting to watch.

Palomino parades, as described in the section about palomino horses, are also one of the most popular attractions at state fairs.

RIDING FOR PLEASURE

The subject of horses at play would not be complete without some mention of the hundreds of horses who contribute to man's pleasure simply by being ridden. On farms, ranches, camps, trails and in parks—whether purebred saddle horses or ordinary nags—these horses give fun and exercise to men, women and children all over the world. Such horses are often family pets that also work as light draft horses or cow ponies. The patience to be learned from their training and companionship does as much to mold a rider's character as riding does to mold his figure.

An amusing bit of riding for the sheer fun of it is done by an organization known as the Desert Caballeros (*caballero* is the Spanish word for horseman). Here some hundred and fifty older business and professional men meet together in Arizona once every year for a five-day ride. Presidents of banks, Wall Street brokers, lawyers and doctors cover about a hundred miles of western plains and hills during these five days, camping out at night. Their "roughing it" is a little different from the average cowboy's, however. Ten trucks go ahead of them to the camp sites, where chefs prepare delicious meals from huge refrigerators. The saddlesore horsemen sleep on air mattresses on the ground, shave with electric razors powered by the truck's generator—and eat dinners of fried chicken and strawberries!

Another group of enthusiastic pleasure riders bears the name of Boycott's Bouncing Belles. This is a group of New Jersey ladies—many of them grandmothers—who ride country trails together under the leadership of a Miss Boycott. They are very particular about their riding habits and their riding form, and they enjoy the sport so much that they have been riding every Wednesday for several years. Some of their saddle horses are twenty years old. Often as many as thirty of the ladies' children and grandchildren ride with them.

But where only a few can ride in luxury like the Desert Caballeros or Bouncing Belles, many thousands get much simple pleasure from their friend, the horse. No matter how mechanical the world of the future becomes, it is to be hoped that the machine will never take the place of this good partner in good fun.

PART 6

Horses Rare and Different

HORSE SENSE IN GENERAL

People who like horses disagree as to the amount of real intelligence they have. Some say the horse learns only from training, habit or memory, and has no reasoning power of his own. In tests conducted at New York City's Bronx Zoo for two years, both the dog and the horse got much *lower* intelligence marks than wild animals did. Scientists believe this is because wild animals had to use their own brains to feed, house or defend themselves before they were captured. But tame animals have depended on man so long for their care that their natural intelligence is not developed as it might have been if they had never been domesticated.

This seems to be proved by the fact that horses who are half wild, or who have a wild ancestry, often show more initiative. Mustang cow ponies, left to run on the range when they aren't being worked, do their work with real independence. And Shetland ponies, whose ancestors for centuries roamed the Scottish hills, still show signs of greater horse sense than many other breeds. On the other hand, Arabian horses who are brought up exceptionally close to man—almost as members of the family—are noted for their smartness.

Some people claim that a horse hasn't got the brains to run out of a burning stable. Others claim that a horse remains in his stall precisely *because* of his intelligence. The stall has come to mean the place of greatest security —in spite of his terror of fire. He feels safer from danger there than anywhere else. Besides, who hasn't heard stories of people who run into a burning building to rescue some silly possessions, only to get badly hurt for their foolishness?

This disagreement about the amount of horse sense a horse really has will probably continue as long as there are horses in the world. But a few general observations seem to be accepted by both sides in the argument:

It seems pretty definite that most of the things a horse does he has learned by training. These he repeats from habit or memory rather than from independent reasoning. It seems fairly certain that no horse can think of more than one thing at a time. It also seems sure, too, that many horses have a sense of humor, which may or may not indicate intelligence. They will nip a cap off a groom's head, drop it into a bucket of water, then look at him with the terrible twinkle of a practical joker in their eyes.

Many horses seem to like music. A man who owned several horses tells of playing some records of Beethoven symphonies outdoors one fine afternoon. At the first notes, all his horses lined up along the fence which separated their pasture from the front yard where the phonograph was. They stood there until the music ended, then cantered happily away.

Horses have definite physical ways of expressing what's on their minds. Since they can't talk our language, however, we have to understand what these physical sounds and motions mean before we can measure how smart the horse is. For example, when a horse points his ears forward and down, giving a short snort as he does so, this may mean "Hey, look what's there!" If he drops one ear forward, holds the other back, while he trots sideways with his head held to the side, he is warning you that he feels full of Old Nick—so you better watch out for what he may do next. Ears thrown back even a very little mean anger. If they are flat back along his neck it means a fighting rage.

Neighing means different things, too. A rumbling sort of grumbling neigh is a demand for food. A soft, low whinny is the love call of a horse for a mare. When passing other horses a cheerful neigh means "Hi!" When in great pain a horse groans very much like a man, even cries tears from his nostrils. A scream is given only when the horse is in unbearable agony.

Movements of feet and body all have different meanings. Stamping just means the horse is impatient, but pawing the ground may mean he's sick. Pointing with the forefoot means something hurts him there. Dragging a forefoot means he's hurt his shoulder. Head hanging down—tail tucked under his body—means he's very sick or suffering from some obscure ache.

When he's happy a horse shows his feelings in many ways. His eyes are bright, his coat glossy, his head carried high and proudly. He nickers at other horses, shies in pretended fright at a piece of paper, leaps in the air just for the fun of it. His nostrils quiver and his ears move constantly. If he feels affectionate he will nuzzle your hand for a petting. These are all ways with which a horse tries to communicate with a human being.

A horse's eyesight is different from ours. Naturally, this affects his actions. He sees very well at six feet, but anything one hundred yards away seems blurred to him. The main purpose of his eyes is to let him see every detail of the surrounding grass, bushes or trees for his food, to inspect every square inch of the ground before him for his safe walking or running. His eyes have a much wider angle of vision than humans' have. He can see forward, sideward and backward. He can also see better than a man in the dark. His sure, careful trot through the night makes him seem very smart, but if one counted on him to see something a mile away he would seem equally dumb.

The horse is thought to have a sense of smell about ten times as acute as a human's. A rider, lost without water for several days on a barren plain, once owed his life to this fact. Although there was no wind to carry a scent, his horse suddenly began to gallop. He galloped for about five miles to a small pond of fresh water. This saved both man and horse from dying of thirst—but was the horse's action due to intelligence? Or was it simply due to the fact that he was thirsty and had been able to scent water long before his rider could?

Many an old-time milk wagon driver can tell of horses that stopped at every customer's door without any signal. And many a country doctor, before automobiles, remembers how he tied up the reins of his buggy after a long-distance call in the middle of the night, then went to

*Some horses are famous for their intelligence or for the
special things they have been taught to do*

sleep while his horse brought him safely home. Did these horses act from reason or habit?

No matter whether such examples were due to horse sense or horse memory, there are some specific horses who have made a reputation because of their special intelligence—or because of the special things they have been trained to do.

Outstanding Horses

One of the most famous groups of outstanding horses are those that belong to the Spanish Riding Academy of Vienna, Austria. They are to the horse world what a great ballet company is to the world of humans—specially trained, beautiful beings who perform difficult but graceful feats for our artistic pleasure. They also serve the purpose of keeping alive an old art of traditional horsemanship and training.

This breed of what were formerly royal horses, called Lippizaners, was founded in 1590. They got their name from the town of Lippiza in what is now Yugoslavia, where they originated. Their ancestors were lovely, graceful Spanish horses, which gave the riding academy its name. The horses used in the earliest days of the Royal Vienna Academy were the same kind that are used today for this disciplined display of riding.

They are milk-white horses with very short, round throats that hold proud heads. Their eyes are deep and dark, their necks curving in an arch. They have long white tails and manes, a strong, broad breast and light, powerful legs which give grace to every step they take.

Like other white horses, they are black when they are born. They turn gray when they are two years old, silver by the time they are three, while at the end of their fourth year they become all white. Only when they reach this age are certain ones selected for the academy and their years of training begin.

Just as the horses and their equipment are the same type as they were in the eighteenth century, so the costumes worn by their riders are the same—black knee boots, white breeches, brown coats with gold buttons—and a boat-shaped hat trimmed with gold braid.

All the "tricks" done by the Lippizan stallions are the same today as they were then, too. Horse trainers carefully watched and studied young colts at play in pastures. They developed the colts' natural leaps, gaits and poses into formal steps which they taught the Lippizaners to perform. These steps have French or German names, such as:

Piaffe: a brisk trot done with the forefeet lifted high and the neck arched. The horse stands in one spot as he trots, never moving an inch ahead.

Redopp: a furious gallop done in a tiny circle no bigger than ten feet across.

Levade: a pose seen in many statues of riders on horseback, where the hind legs are bent close to the ground, with the forelegs arched high in the air. The horse holds this pose for many seconds.

Courbette: here the horse stands on his hind legs, forelegs raised close to his chest, then jumps forward

158

in this position in a series of hops, without ever touching his forefeet to the earth.

Capriole: this step is considered the peak of riding art, and only Lippizaners have ever been able to do it. The horse pulls his four legs together under him just as he leaps high into the air. At the top of the leap he suddenly throws his legs out in a straight line, making a beautiful momentary picture before he lands on the ground.

At performances, the Spanish horses display these and other tricks, then end by doing a sort of quadrille—a formal dance in which the music keeps perfect time to their steps while the riders guide them in various patterns. It takes years of patient teaching by some of Europe's greatest horsemen to train horses to do these difficult, lovely things. Riders come from all over the world to study at the academy. They learn not only how to train horses, but how to improve their own riding. Groups of the Spanish Riding Academy's horses have exhibited their art in many countries, including the United States. They are a very special joy for any horse lover to watch.

There have been many unusual individual horses in many countries. During Queen Anne's reign in England, there was a horse called the best-trained horse in the world. He often performed for the Queen in her palace. He is said to have been able to fetch and carry like a dog. If one hid a handkerchief, a penny or a glove in a room, the horse hunted until he found the small object and brought it to his master. He could also tell the number of spots on a card, they say, and jump through a hoop.

Queenie, a Shetland pony owned by a minister in Massachusetts, loved to eat cigarettes. She would sidle up to a strange man and steal a cigarette from his pocket before he knew what was happening. She could also untie knots in ropes, slide bolts on a door to open it, lift door latches when she wanted to go out—and open gates. As far as anyone knew, she had never been trained to do any of these things. She simply taught herself.

Another Shetland pony, Black Bear, was the cause of much discussion by scientists. He could spell sentences or give numbers by moving lettered or numbered tabs that hung on a rack before him. He could give a correct "yes" or "no" answer to questions by motions of his head. He told time from a watch and made the right change from a lot of coins. Since his master always insisted on being with him when he showed off these tricks, it was suspected that he gave Black Bear secret, hidden signals so he could give the correct answers.

Another big debate arose in Germany, in 1904, over whether or not a Russian stallion named Hans could do mathematical problems, spell words, tell the time or the date of the month, pick out different objects by their color. Many university professors took sides in the debate, observing Hans at work and reporting their findings. Some scientists believed Hans followed certain unconscious movements made by his trainer when he ordered Hans to do something. Others decided that Hans really and truly had the ability to reason out these unbelievable tricks for himself.

A French professor owned two Arabian stallions named Muhamed and Zarif. They solved problems in numbers that were written on a blackboard in their stall. No one was present to direct them either by conscious or unconscious signs, and observers watched the horses at work through two hidden windows. Apparently Muhamed and Zarif moved numbered or lettered blocks with their feet to solve mathematical problems and to spell out words. They used strange spelling that no man would have taught them. The story goes that one day the professor went into Muhamed's stall. The horse at once spelled out for him in the blocks the message, "Albert has beaten Hanschen." And Albert, who was a groom in the stable, had indeed beaten Hanschen—a Shetland pony—that very day!

Remarkable as such things seem, no one has ever agreed on the reasons for them. Nor do all students of the subject believe they really happened. It will probably take many years and countless more experiments before they actually know for sure whether horses are as capable of independent thinking as such incidents seem to indicate. But since scientists do agree that horses can do almost anything they have been *trained* to do, this chapter about rare and different horses ends with the story of Gaylord:

Gaylord is an eight-year-old chestnut horse whose home is in Louisville, Kentucky. He has been taught to drive an automobile! True, the car has been specially constructed for him. Gaylord stands in a sort of stall where the back seat of an open car would normally be. A large brake pedal made of wood is near his left front hoof. Another large pedal, covered with rubber, is near his right front hoof. This is the accelerator. The steering wheel has a long rod which lets it reach up right before

Gaylord's nose, while the gearshift, too, has been made much higher.

Gaylord pulls a lever with his teeth to start the motor. Using his teeth again, he puts the car into gear by shifting the gearshift. He steps on the accelerator with his right hoof and steers with his nose on the steering wheel. It has taken him three years to learn to do these things. He seldom goes faster than four miles an hour, however, and his trainer always rides in a near-by car to tell him just what to do and when to do it. But even so, it must be a remarkable sight to see Gaylord drive off in his automobile alone!

PART 7

Horses and You

So You Want to Own a Horse!

There's a saying that goes, "The outside of a horse is good for the inside of a man." Anyone who has ever ridden will agree, for this particular exercise in the fresh air strengthens the body while it sharpens physical and mental alertness. It does even more than that. The self-discipline needed to care for, train, ride and control a horse is as good for character as the exercise is good for muscles. But there are three principal errors which a person must correct if he really wants to get the most enjoyment from his horse. These errors are:

1. To show fear to a horse
2. To show meanness or neglect in caring for him
3. To show cruelty or bad temper in handling him

It's easy to see that conquering such faults will not only make a horse happier, but will also make his rider a more self-controlled and a more thoughtful human

Having your own horse is a wonderful experience

being. This must be one important reason why there are still so many of these pets in the world today, in spite of the expense of owning a horse and the popularity of other sports.

If you are that lucky girl or boy who already has your own horse, you have probably learned to do all the things a person your age *can* do in caring for him. But if you haven't a pony and hope to get one someday, the following pages may help you to handle him, although you obviously can't take complete care of such a large animal. You will have to rely on riding instructors, blacksmiths, veterinarians and other grownups for the more complicated problems of riding, health, housing, feeding and grooming. But there are certain simple things you can learn to do which will make both you and your pet realize that he is *your* horse.

After an experienced adult has selected the right kind of healthy horse for you, whether a purebred or a crossbreed, you will want to give it a name. Suppose you have been given a lovely little chestnut mare, because mares are gentle with children and easily trained. She has such a gay sparkle in hr eyes and such a light way of moving over the ground—almost as if she were flying—that you decide to call her Tinker, after Tinker Bell in *Peter Pan*.

Before you bring Tinker home from her stable, you will make her acquaintance by talking to her softly before you touch her. Perhaps you offer her a carrot to nibble, so she'll begin to learn that you are her friend. The next thing you have to do is to be sure that Tinker has the right kind of house to live in when she becomes part of your family.

This house need not be fancy or expensive—as long as it meets certain requirements. The stable should be light, dry, clean and protected from direct drafts of cold air. Tinker should be kept in a stall in the stable, as this lets her move around freely without being tied. The stall should be about twelve feet square and have a dirt or clay floor that can easily be replaced. Straw makes a good bed for her, although wood shavings are sometimes used. Feeding bins are placed at one end of the stall—a separate one for hay and another for grain. The stall should be cleaned every day with a stiff broom. A pitchfork is used to remove the old bedding when you want to put in fresh straw. About twice a year the stall should be washed down with disinfectant to remove any possible germs or disagreeable odors. Some powdered limestone sprinkled on the floor each day will keep the stable sweet smelling.

If you live on a farm or ranch, such a home for Tinker can easily be made in one corner of the barn. If you live in a small town, where you have no barn, you can rent a building on the outskirts. Or maybe you can get together with other boys and girls who have horses—all of you chipping in to pay the rent on a stable for all your ponies. If you live in a large city, however, you can board Tinker in a near-by public stable. Just be sure to inspect the stall you rent to see that it meets all the requirements mentioned above.

Tinker's Diet

After a proper home has been prepared you should learn something about the proper food for Tinker. Like humans, horses need to eat the right things in order to be healthy. An experienced horse breeder or a veterinarian will probably help your parents decide on the best diet for Tinker, since each horse has to be fed according to his temperament and the amount of work he does. But here are some general rules you might like to know:

1. Feed Tinker at regular hours. She may get fretful if you are late with her dinner.

2. Give Tinker more grain and less hay when she has been exercising a lot. Give her less grain and more hay if she's been lazing around her stall all day.

3. Give her plenty of water often, unless she's hot.

4. Change her diet little by little, so her stomach won't become upset by too sudden changes.

166

5. Keep a lump of rock salt always handy in her stall.

6. If you have a pasture for her to run in—and haven't been able to ride her—let Tinker out to eat and exercise.

Here are some sample menus for a light horse like Tinker, who weighs around a thousand pounds:

One day's feed might consist of seven pounds of oats, two pounds of wheat bran, eight pounds of timothy hay and four pounds of alfalfa or clover hay. Another dinner might consist of seven pounds of oats, one pound of yellow corn, half a pound of linseed meal or soybean meal, ten pounds of timothy and two pounds of alfalfa or clover. Or if Tinker has been out to pasture all day, you might see that she gets six pounds of oats and eight pounds of timothy in addition to the grass she has been nibbling.

Don't forget that lots of water is essential to her good health, but remember the important rule of never watering her when she's overheated. It doesn't matter if you water her before her meal, during it or afterward. Just decide which you will do, then do it regularly.

For an occasional dessert, or as a reward for good behavior, a carrot, a turnip or an apple will make Tinker mighty happy. And all horses love sugar. A few lumps once in a while won't spoil Tinker's teeth or figure, but don't give her too much.

TINKER'S GOOD LOOKS

Grooming a horse is as important to her comfort as it is to her appearance. A horse sheds her coat in the spring and in the fall, so daily brushing helps remove the old hair and makes the coat glossy. It also prevents the development of skin disorders. Here's what you can learn to do yourself in this matter of grooming:

First, remember to *walk* Tinker during the last fifteen minutes of a ride, so she returns to her stall cool and dry instead of hot and wet. Next, when you're sure she's dry, unsaddle her and go over her body with a brush in one hand and a rubber comb in the other. Start at her head and work back with circular motions. You can then go over her again with a soft, dry cloth. Last, wash out her nostrils and eyes—and around her tail—with a damp sponge. If you want to groom her mane and tail, pick out snarls or burrs with your fingers. Then brush lightly so you don't pull out too many hairs.

Water is seldom used to clean a horse's body, as it makes the hair harsh and dull. Regular daily brushing will keep her clean. When you want Tinker to look especially glamorous, however, a rubdown with olive oil will give her coat a splendid sheen.

If Tinker should be hot after an outing, you can rub her down with rubbing alcohol, especially on the part of her back that has been under the saddle. Then lead her in a slow walk around the yard until she is thoroughly cool and dry before you give her a drink of water or bed her down in her stall. If she's had a very hard workout and her legs seem stiff and tired, you can rub them down with a liniment recommended by a veterinarian.

Whenever you unsaddle Tinker you should carefully inspect her body and legs for possible blisters or sores— and tell your vet about them so he can prescribe the right treatment. You should also make it a habit to inspect her feet for possible stones, injury or cracked heels. Take her to a good blacksmith for correct shoes when they are needed. A good hint for dry weather—to prevent Tinker's feet from drying out too much—is to put a handful of mud on the bottom of each hoof after a ride.

The story of a race horse who began to lose all his races proves the value of this hint. When his owner failed to find what was causing him to lose so often, he put the horse out to rest on a farm. He began to notice that the horse left the good grass of the fields to go and stand for hours in a near-by swamp. It was only then that the owner realized all the horse's trouble lay in his feet—and he had found his own best medicine. When the horse began to spend more time in the grass and less time in the swamp, the owner decided he was ready to race again. Taking some barrels of mud along to keep the horse's hoofs damp and cool, he entered his animal in races—many of which he then won.

TINKER'S WARDROBE

In addition to keeping his horse well groomed, a good horseman also sees to it that his tack is always clean and shining. "Tack" is the word for the leather, metal and cloth equipment that Tinker wears—her wardrobe of girth, saddle, stirrups, bridle, reins and blankets.

Your parents will have bought you the best tack they can afford—and no matter how simple this is, it adds up to quite a bit of money. Therefore, to keep it in condition so it will last a long time, it should be cleaned after every ride. To do a good job of this you should have at hand a bucket of warm water, sponges, a chamois skin (called a "shammy"), soft soap, neats-foot oil, either glycerin or saddle soap, metal polish, clean rags and a clothesbrush or whisk broom.

First, hang the saddle blanket out to dry while you start to work on the saddle itself. Remove the girth and stirrups, unbuckling all buckles, then wash the leather with warm water, a sponge and soft soap. Dry it with the shammy. Now rub it with a damp sponge dipped in the glycerin or saddle soap, paying particular attention to the undersides of the flaps. Let the saddle dry while you sponge and dry the bridle, stirrup leathers, girth and reins, then rub them with a little neats-foot oil. Wash and wipe the bit and stirrups, but don't polish them with the metal cleaner. They are made of steel or nickle and don't need it. Do polish, however, any brass buckles that may be tarnished. Now go back to your saddle and rub it to a hard finish with a clean cloth. Brush the blanket thoroughly with the clothesbrush. Put each article back in its place in the stable—and you're all ready for your next ride.

A light sponging with neats-foot oil on the inside of the girth and the saddle flaps will help keep them soft and pliable so they won't irritate Tinker's skin. If you haven't used your tack for so long that the leather has become hard and dry, you can rub into it a mixture of half lanolin and half neats-foot oil. This will give it new life.

You Learn to Ride Tinker

It's impossible to learn how to ride a horse from reading a book. Once you have Tinker, however, you will probably also be lucky enough to know some adult who will give you actual lessons in this art. For a long time experts have agreed that the earlier a youngster started to learn to ride, the better horseman he would grow up to be. During the Golden Age of Athens there was a law which required every single Greek boy of twelve years old to own, ride and care for a horse. And among the most popular entries in today's horse shows are the pony classes which are ridden or driven by young girls and boys.

While it's true you can't learn to ride from a book, there are some general pointers which may help you learn more easily from experience. The first pointer is for you to know your horse.

You must not show any fear of Tinker, even if you *are* afraid of her, since Tinker will sense this at once and become nervous or fearful herself. If you are too bold, on the other hand, you must learn caution so that you will harm neither yourself nor your precious pet—out of reckless ignorance. The best approach to Tinker is one of respect for her strength, her intelligence and her nerves. If you train yourself to have a quiet, gentle, but confident, manner, no matter how you really feel, then you will also have a quiet, gentle, but confident, mount.

Tinker is brave and has great eagerness to please you, once she understands what you want her to do. It is this anxiety to please, this confidence that you know what you're asking her to do, which make her obedient even when she may be nervous or frightened. Once you understand this, you'll see there is no reason to be afraid of her —yet every reason to respect her confidence in you. If you have younger brothers or sisters who want to do the right thing, yet are a little excitable, watch how your parents handle them. This is the way you should learn to handle Tinker.

Before you actually get up on her back for the first time, however, you should spend some hours getting to know her better. Visit the stable to watch her being groomed and bridled. Learn to go up to her stall in a way that is neither so loud and boisterous that she's alarmed, nor so quiet and sneaky that you startle her. Talk to her for a while before you pet her. Offer her a carrot or an apple tidbit on the flat of your hand. Pat her first on the neck—not the head—then on the nose. Little by little, she will let you touch her head and ears.

See how carefully the groom turns her in the stall when he wants her to go out. This is so she won't knock against anything or slip on the floor. Watch how he takes a rein in each hand, close to the bit, and walks backward in front of her to lead her out of the stall. This is done so she won't bang into the door or walls of the stable. A groom will also show you how to saddle Tinker, as this is something you'll have to learn from actually handling a saddle, girth and stirrups. No book can help you here!

Up You Get!

At last you feel you know Tinker well enough—and she knows you well enough—for the big moment when you can get up on her back for the first time. But—that's easier said than done! Your legs are so short that Tinker's back seems to be way up in the air over your head. Even using a mounting block or steps, how will you ever get up there safely?

172

Maybe you'd better postpone mounting Tinker until you've practiced mounting a saddled dummy horse. Everything you do with the dummy you'll do later with Tinker. She'll stand still patiently because she's a very polite and understanding horse. She'll never show surprise at even your clumsiest antics as you try to scramble into the saddle.

But let's try the dummy first. You stand facing the saddle, near the dummy's front legs. Now you must adjust the length of the stirrup leathers to suit the length of your legs. The way to do this is to hold the stirrup iron with your right hand in the pit of your left arm. Then straighten your left arm along the leather, holding your left hand in a loose fist. When your arm is stiff and straight your knuckles should just touch the stirrup bar— that piece of metal which holds the stirrup leather to the saddle. If they don't touch, you then adjust the buckles to make the leather longer. If your knuckles touch too much, then shorten the leather. Measure again until it's exactly right for you. This is very important.

You are now ready to mount the dummy from its near, or left, side. Staying by its front legs, you face its rear legs. Holding the reins in your left hand, rest that hand on the dummy's left shoulder just in front of the saddle. Throw the long ends of the reins over to the other side, clear of the saddle so you won't sit on them. The reins should be held rather short in order to prevent Tinker from turning her head when you get around to mounting her.

Next, take the stirrup leather in your right hand, twist it so it is facing forward, then place your left foot in the stirrup. Hop around until you are facing the dummy.

173

Your left toe should dig into the girth, not into the dummy's side.

Now, with the left hand still holding the reins, grasp the pommel of the saddle. Take hold of the pommel with your right hand, too, as far to the off side as you can reach. Spring up on your right toes at the same time you straighten your left leg. This will bring you to a standing position in the left stirrup. Throw your right leg over the dummy's back and seat yourself gently in the saddle. Try not to land with a bump. Now place your right foot in its stirrup—and you've mounted your horse.

You won't do all this correctly the first few times you try, but each attempt will be easier. Eventually you will mount and find your right stirrup with your foot without looking down for it.

The Seat

The seat, or the proper way to sit on a horse, is the next thing you should learn. Your instructor won't be as severe as the instructors at the Spanish Riding Academy of Vienna. There, young riders are trained with a long rod of iron fastened inside their jackets, down their spines, so they *have* to sit erect. However, if you can manage to acquire a seat that enables you to stay in the saddle—without hanging onto the reins or gripping with your legs—that will be a good beginning.

First you must find the correct place to sit on the saddle. That place is the very lowest part of the saddle: neither way forward nor way back but right in the middle. If your stirrups are the proper length, your legs will be slightly bent at the knees. The very tips of your toes should be about in line with the points of your knees. Your heels will be sunk down and the balls of your feet will press on the stirrup irons.

As you learn to ride you will also learn to use the inner muscles of the calves of your legs to guide Tinker. You will keep your knees snug against the saddle, your toes slightly out and not too deep in the stirrups. Your back will be straight but never stiff, since your body must be relaxed and ready to balance itself with the movements of the horse. Your head will be up, your chin in, your eyes fixed straight ahead between Tinker's ears. You will hold your arms close to your sides, keeping the elbows in, while your hands and wrists will learn how to do their special job with the reins.

A nice, easy, correct seat is something you may have to work hard to acquire, but once you have it it will stay with you all your riding days. There's a well-known little saying that might help you remember the most important things about how to sit a horse:

> "The head and the heart keep up,
> The hands and the heels keep down,
> The elbows and the knees keep in."

THE HANDS

In good riding, next in importance to the seat are the hands. The hands hold the reins, while the reins are attached to the bit in Tinker's mouth. The slightest pressure on the reins is transferred into pressure on her mouth. This is how she is trained to obey your instructions. Too much pressure on the bit can be painful, however, and it is terribly important never to cause Tinker any unnecessary pain. Pain is perhaps the cause of more accidents or runaways than any other single thing. So aside from the fact that you don't want to hurt your pet, it is safer for *you* if she isn't hurt.

If you imagine the reins as being very thin, fragile lines made of silk, you will use them correctly to guide—but not to yank—Tinker. You will hold the reins in both hands, one rein going between the little and the third fingers of your left hand, the other going between the little and the third fingers of your right hand. The fingers should be slightly closed and both hands should be held an inch above the pommel, at your waist level, and about four inches apart. Your wrists should always be relaxed, not stiff. They will act like springs in manipulating the reins when you begin to lead Tinker through her various paces.

With practice, you'll be able to shorten reins when necessary. You'll also get the "feel" of Tinker's mouth so you'll know exactly how much pressure to exert in order to tell her what to do—without frightening or hurting her. You'll always keep your hands down . . . never even have to look at them to see what they're doing with the reins.

AIDS

Aids are the ways a rider conveys his wishes to his mount to persuade him to do what he wants him to do.

Such aids are the hands, the legs, the voice, and the body. You will find that your hands control the reins which put Tinker's head in the direction you want her to go. Your legs exert pressure on Tinker's sides that tells her how fast or how slowly you want her to move.

Your voice is still another aid, but a good rider does not use words like "whoa" or "giddap." These instructions are given silently, by means of other aids. The voice is used only to reassure Tinker if she's startled, or to order her to back up. The tone is always a gentle one, never a loud command. The body is another aid which influences the horse by a shift of weight from forward to back, or to one side, depending on what you want her to do.

Whips, spurs and other mechanical devices are called "artificial aids." They should be used only long after you have become an accomplished horseman, if at all.

The Different Gaits

The three principal gaits have already been mentioned earlier in this book. These are probably the first ones your instructor will teach you. They are the walk, the trot and the canter. Later, you might also learn to ride a five-gaited horse with his extra gaits of running walk and rack. And while a gallop is not required of a saddle horse in a show, it is a natural gait for any horse and one you should learn to control.

As with all riding—from saddling and mounting to dismounting—you simply cannot learn how to manage the different gaits from reading about them. The best that can be attempted here is to give you some hints that may help you understand your teacher's instructions when you're actually up on Tinker.

The Walk

Before Tinker is asked to obey any order she must first be "collected." This means she will be well balanced on her four feet, with her head up, ready to do whatever you tell her. An "uncollected" horse stands with head hanging and a lazy indifference to the world. To expect a horse is this position to obey you gracefully and immediately is rather like expecting a boy to make a clean start in a race when he's standing on the side lines eating an ice-cream cone. The boy must be on his mark and set before he can go. And so Tinker must "get set" before she can start out—even on the slowest possible walk.

Once mounted, therefore, you collect Tinker by a pressure of your legs and a feel of the reins pulling gently on her bit. Her head comes up, her weight is evenly balanced and she is ready for anything. To ask her to walk, you then ease the reins and at the same time keep the same leg pressure. You relax this pressure as soon as she's moving steadily.

In a walk, Tinker's head will bob a little with each step, so you must "give" in your arms and wrists to keep the correct pressure on the reins. If she stretches her head down, give enough rein to permit this. Then immediately bring her head back to the riding position by shortening the reins. You'll know by the position of her head whether you're holding the reins too slack or too short. If slack, her head will be too low and her walk

Horses' gaits: Top row, left to right—walk, trot. Bottom row, left to right—canter, gallop

sloppy. If short, her head will be too high and her walk choppy. In a good walk you hear the four distinct beats of four hoofs, one after the other, in a steady rhythm as they hit the ground.

Your instructor will have to teach you to turn and back Tinker, but you might like to know now how to stop her! Close both legs against your saddle and pull evenly (do not *yank*) on the reins. At the same time, ease the weight of your body toward the back of the saddle. Tinker should come to a clean, collected stop—and then you can relax both the pressure of your legs and the pull on the reins.

The Trot

Just as a baby has to learn how to walk before he can run, you'll have to learn how to trot before you can canter. This is too bad, in a way, since many people find it harder to trot correctly than to canter. But the necessity of learning to trot will help you learn the other gaits all the more easily. Start by practicing a few minutes at a time so your muscles don't get stiff. Here's what you do, in general:

Tinker is walking. To tell her to trot, close both legs behind the girth and ease both reins a little. You may at the same time grasp her mane well forward or touch her neck with your hand. At once, from a pleasant walk, you will find yourself bumping up and down in the saddle as Tinker begins to trot with the left front foot and the right hind foot moving at the same time. Then the right front foot moves with the left hind foot. Before you learn to rise to the trot, however, you will hit the saddle with a thump each time Tinker's two opposite feet hit the ground.

Since this is painful for both horse and rider, the sooner you learn to rise in the saddle when trotting, the more comfortable you'll both be. The way to avoid the bump is to lift your weight slightly off the saddle just as Tinker's right front foot and left hind foot leave the ground, sinking down into the saddle when they land.

This is the principle of rising to the trot, or posting. With a good teacher, plenty of patience and some practice, you'll soon forget your saddle-thumping days and be trotting merrily on your way.

The Canter

The canter is a slow gallop—with a sort of rocking chair motion that is very pleasant. You should always canter Tinker on soft ground, never on a road, and you should keep her collected at a steady pace, not too fast, to prevent her from breaking into a gallop.

You do not rise to a canter as you do to a trot. You may rise without meaning to, however, until you've learned the trick. But once your body finds its balance and rhythm, you'll be sitting as firmly in your saddle as if you were in a chair. In the canter both Tinker's front feet leave the ground at the same time in a slight spring. The leading forefoot hits the ground first, followed by the opposite hind foot, then both remaining feet hit the ground together. This gives a one-two-three beat, with the heavy accent on three. This description may sound complicated, but the canter is really a pleasant gait to ride. You will soon learn to sit down and forward in your saddle, elbows in, reins giving enough for Tinker's head to move back and forward, yet held firmly enough so she doesn't begin to gallop.

The Gallop

If you should want a quick run, you tell Tinker to move from a canter into a gallop by leg pressure and an easing up on the reins. But you should never give Tinker her head. This means you should always have her under your control—going at the speed you wish. You must never allow the reins to be so slack that Tinker just dashes off across the country as fast as she wishes—to any destination she wishes.

In the gallop, Tinker's two front feet leave the ground practically together. Then, just an instant before they hit the ground, the two hind feet come up. For a second, all four feet are in the air. Then the front feet land, followed by the rear feet. The beat is a steady one-two.

Your seat for a gallop can be the same as for a canter, but with the knees and thighs gripping the saddle more tightly. Or you may crouch forward, putting your weight on your knees, thighs and stirrups rather than on your saddle. If you ride this way, you will shorten your reins so as to maintain a firm feel of Tinker's mouth, thus keeping her under control so she doesn't run away.

Down You Get!

There are several acceptable ways of dismounting. They are called the vault, the roll—in which the stirrups are used—and the side.

Your teacher will train you in the style he prefers, but the method probably used most frequently is with the stirrups. In dismounting this way, you simply reverse the order of the steps you used in mounting.

Holding the reins in your left hand with enough pressure to keep Tinker standing still, you free your right foot from its stirrup. Lean forward and put both hands on the pommel. Then swing your right leg over the back of the horse. As soon as your right toe touches the ground —on Tinker's left side—take your right hand off the pommel. You will be facing Tinker's rear legs, standing on your right foot with your left foot still in its stirrup. Release your left foot and you'll be on the ground again, the reins still held in your left hand.

As you become more expert, you'll probably learn to take your left foot from its stirrup at the moment your right foot swings over Tinker's back, jumping to the ground on both feet at once.

Your Riding Habit

Unless you expect to exhibit Tinker in a horse show some day, there is no reason why your riding clothes need be expensive. There are certain rather rigid rules of dress for riders in a show, but these need not concern you right now.

While your habit doesn't have to be fancy for daily riding, it should follow along a few common-sense lines, starting with your underwear. To prevent possible chafing or soreness from unnecessary wrinkles in the cloth, your underpants should fit snugly without either binding or bagging. Next in importance to your comfort are the breeches. These can be of a formal riding habit cut, which must be worn with jack boots, laced boots or leggings. Or they can be cut in the jodhpur style, which can be worn with low jodhpur boots or oxfords. Or they can be blue jeans tucked into the tops of low cowboy-type boots or rolled over their tops. Or they can be any other type of pants you like—as long as they come down to your ankles.

Shorts are definitely *not* recommended because your bare legs can be too easily chafed by the saddle.

Wear a polo shirt or a cotton sports shirt if the weather is warm, or add a jacket or sweater if the weather turns cold. A jockey-type cap will keep both your hair and the sun out of your eyes—and look smart, besides. In cold or wet weather you may want to wear gloves. Choose string gloves a size larger than you usually wear. They are better than leather ones because they won't slip on the reins.

FUN WITH TINKER

The time will come when you'll be so much at home on Tinker's back, whether trotting, cantering or galloping, that you'll begin to look for other ways of having fun on horseback. Perhaps you'll want to jump, starting over low, wide sacks filled with earth or straw, then graduating to fences and hedges. If you enjoy this kind of riding you might want to have a paper chase.

In a paper chase you get together several riding friends and their mounts—then select one to be "it." This leader starts alone across country on his horse, strewing bits of paper from a bag attached to his saddle as he rides. After he has disappeared from sight for a few moments, all the rest of you start after him, following the paper trail as fast as your horses will carry you. The first one to follow the trail back "home" wins the chase.

When you have learned to be real fast and slippery at getting on and off Tinker, you might arrange a game of musical chairs with your fellow riders. This is played just like the parlor game in the house—only instead of chairs

184

You can have fun with your horse in many ways

you place low wooden boxes around a large circle out of doors. You have one less box than there are players. Then, when the "referee" starts some music on a record-player, every rider rides around the circle—keeping his eye on the boxes. As soon as the music stops he dashes wildly for the nearest box, jumps off his horse and stands on the box. The player left without a box leaves the game, while one box is also removed. The game continues until a single rider wins by getting to the last box first.

If the rest of your family likes to ride, too, you can arrange horseback picnics, carrying your lunch as you follow trails through the woods and fields. If you live in the wide open spaces of the West, you'll probably race your friends across the plains—or learn to do some plain roping tricks. There are all sorts of things you'll find to do with Tinker. Depending upon where you live and what your special interests are, you'll learn to do best those things that appeal to you most—hunting, point-to-point racing, rounding up cattle, exhibiting at a local fair or horse show, or just plain riding around looking at the world.

And on days when the weather won't permit you to ride, or you're home with the sniffles, you can still have fun with your interest in horses. Why not start a scrapbook the very day you get Tinker? You can fill it full of snapshots of Tinker and yourself as you learn to ride. You can collect magazine pictures of different breeds of horses, news articles about rare things done by rare horses, stories of famous horses and the different deeds or kind of work they do. If you also keep a sort of diary about Tinker and you—what you learned from each other, things you've seen and done during a ride—you might find this a great joy to read and reread during indoor days and even long after you've grown up.

Only with such a record of the small details of your time together can you truly relive the wonderful fun and remember the wonderful qualities that made Tinker such a beloved companion.

Anderson, C. W., *Heads Up, Heels Down*. New York: The Macmillan Co., 1944

Anderson, C. W., *Horses Are Folks*. New York: The Macmillan Co., 1950

Brewster, Benjamin, *The First Book of Cowboys*. New York: Franklin Watts, Inc., 1950

Durrell, H. W., *A Manual for Riders*. New York: Ziff-Davis, 1949

Lewis, Benjamin, *Riding*. New York: Garden City Books, 1938

McMeekin, McLennan, *The First Book of Horses*. New York: Franklin Watts, Inc., 1949

Reynolds, James, *A World of Horses*. New York: Creative Age Press, 1947

Rooks, C. F., *Light Horses*. New York: Ziff-Davis, 1946

Stong, Phil, *Horses and Americans*. New York: Frederick Stokes, 1939

Vernon, Arthur, *The History and Romance of the Horse*. New York: Halcyon House, 1941

United States Government Publications

Write to the U. S. Printing Office, Washington, D. C. Give name and number of pamphlets desired, enclosing cost of each.

Breaking and training of colts:	A 1.9:1368	10¢
Breeds of Draft Horses:	A 1.9:619	10¢
Care and Management of Farm Work Horses:	A 1.9:1419	10¢
Feeding Horses:	A 1.9:1030	10¢

INDEX

Alexander the Great, 20–21
Almost breeds, 72–80
  Hunters, 73–74
  Mustangs, 74–77
  Palominos, 78–80
  Polo ponies, 77–78
Almost horses, 80–86
  Donkeys, 80–82
  Mules, 82–84
  Zebras, 84–86
America, the horse in, 26–30
American saddle horses, 50–55
Arabian breed, 56–60

Barbs, 26
Bareback riding, 139–141
Battle horses, 26
Bedouins, 56–58
Belgian breed, 38–39
Black Bear (Shetland pony), 160
Books to read, 187
Breeds of horses, 37–86
  Almost breeds, 72–80
  Almost horses, 80–86
  Heavy draft breeds, 38–45
  Slender and rapid breeds, 50–72
  Tough and shaggy breeds, 45–50

Broncos, 74, 143–145
Bucephalus, 20–21
Burrights, Mrs. Forrest, 137–138

Calf-roping, 143
Calumet Farms, 131
Canadian "Mounties," 115–116
Canalboat horses, 93–94
Canter, 181
Chargers, 23–24
Chariot races, 117–118
Circus horses, 138–142
Citation, 131
City horses today, 116
Clydesdale breed, 40–41
Coach horses, 94–98
Conestoga horse, 91–93
Cortes, Hernando, 26–27
Coursers, 24–25
Cow horses, 106–110
Crossbreds, 37–38

Dawn horse, 15–17
Derby, 129
De Soto, Hernando, 26–28
Dictionary of terms, 31–36
Diet for your horse, 166–167
Dismounting, 182–183

189

Donkeys, 80–82
Draft breeds, 38–45

Eohippus, 15–17
Epsom Downs, 129

Fairs, 145–149
Farm horses, 104–106
Fire horses, 111–113
Fox hunting, 125–128

Gaits, 52, 177–182
  Canter, 181
  Gallop, 181–182
  Trot, 180–181
  Walk, 178–180
Gallop, 181–182
Gaylord (chestnut horse), 161–162
Genghis Khan, 21–22
Goldsmith Maid, 136
Griffith, Dick, 144

Hackney breed, 60–62
Hambletonian, 67–68
Hands, how to use, 175–176
Hans (Russian stallion), 160
Harness racing, 134–138
Heavy draft breeds, 38–45
  Belgian, 38–39
  Clydesdale, 40–41
  Percheron, 41–43
  Shire, 43–44
Horse Talk, 31–36
Horses as food, 18–19
Horses at Play, 117–151
  Chariot horses, 117–118
  Circus horses, 138–142
  Fox hunting, 125–128
  Harness racing, 134–138

Horse shows and state fairs, 145–149
  Polo, 119–122
  Racing, 128–134
  Rodeos, 142–145
  Steeplechases, 123–125
Horses at Work, 87–116
  Canalboat horses, 93–94
  Coach horses, 94–98
  Conestoga horses, 91–93
  Cow horses, 106–110
  Farm horses, 104–106
  Fire horses, 111–113
  Police horses, 113–116
  Pony Express, 100–103
  Trail and pack horses, 89–91
  Train and streetcar horses, 98–100
  War horses, 87–88
Hunters, 73–74
Hunting, 125–128

Indians and their horses, 28–30
Intelligence in horses, 152–162

Java trails, 91

Knights and their horses, 22–25

Learning to ride, 170–183
Lippizan breed, 157–159
Lucas, Tad, 144

Midnight (a bronco), 144–145
Mongolian ponies, 21–22
Morgan breed, 62–64
Mounting your horse, 172–174
Muhamed and Zarif (Arabian stallions), 160–161

190

Mules, 82–84
Mustangs, 74–77

Names of horses, 134
National Horse Show, 146–148
Norwegian Dun breed, 46–47

Outstanding horses, 157–162

Pacing races, 134–138
Pack horses, 89–91
Palfreys, 24
Palominos, 78–80
Parts of the horse (diagram), 32
Percheron breed, 41–43
Point-to-point racing, 74
Police horses, 113–116
Polo, 119–122
Polo ponies, 77–78
Ponies, 47–48
Pony Express, 100–103
Przhevalskis, 45–46
Purebreds, 37

Quarter horses, 64–66
Queenie (Shetland pony), 160

Racing, 128–134
Rapid breeds, 50–72
    American saddle horses, 50–55
    Arabians, 56–60
    Hackneys, 60–62
    Morgans, 62–64
    Quarter horses, 64–66
    Standardbreds, 66–69
    Tennessee walking horses, 69–71
    Thoroughbreds, 71–72

Rare and different horses, 152–162
Riding for pleasure, 149–151
Riding habit, 183–184
Rodeos, 142–145
Royal Northwest Mounted Police, 115–116

Saddle horses, 50–55
Seat, 174–175
Shaggy breeds, 45–50
    Norwegian Duns, 46–47
    Shetland ponies, 47–50
    Wild horses of Asia, 45–46
Shepard, Alma, 138
Shetland ponies, 47–50
Shire breed, 43–44
Shows and fairs, 145–149
Slender breeds, 50–72
    American saddle horses, 50–55
    Arabians, 56–60
    Hackneys, 60–62
    Morgans, 62–64
    Quarter horses, 64–66
    Standardbreds, 66–69
    Tennessee walking horses, 69–71
    Thoroughbreds, 71–72

Spanish Riding Academy, Vienna, 157–159
Sporting horses. SEE: Horses at Play
Stagecoaches, 94–98
Standardbreds, 66–69, 135–137
State fairs, 145–149
Steeplechases, 123–125
Streetcar horses, 98–100
Suffolk breed, 45

191

Tack, 169–170
Tartar ponies, 21–22
Tennessee walking horses, 69–71
Thoroughbreds, 71–72, 133–134
Tough breeds, 45–50
    Norwegian Duns, 46–47
    Shetland ponies, 47–50
    Wild horses of Asia, 45–46
Trail and pack horses, 89–91
Train horses, 98–100
Training your horse, 163–186
Trotting, 180–181
Trotting horses, 66–67

Trotting races, 134–138

Valiant (a donkey), 81
Viennese horses, 157–159

Walking gait, 178–180
War horses, 20–26, 87–88
Wild horses of Asia, 45–46
Working horses. SEE: Horses at Work

Zarif (Arabian stallion), 160–161
Zebras, 84–86

EGYPTIAN

ASSYRIAN

ROMAN

MONGOLIAN

KNIGHT

ARABIAN